RHYME'S CHALLENGE

RHYME'S CHALLENGE

Hip Hop, Poetry, and Contemporary Rhyming Culture

DAVID CAPLAN

OXFORD
UNIVERSITY PRESS

OXFORD
UNIVERSITY PRESS

Oxford University Press is a department of the University of Oxford.
It furthers the University's objective of excellence in research, scholarship,
and education by publishing worldwide.

Oxford   New York
Auckland   Cape Town   Dar es Salaam   Hong Kong   Karachi
Kuala Lumpur   Madrid   Melbourne   Mexico City   Nairobi
New Delhi   Shanghai   Taipei   Toronto

With offices in
Argentina   Austria   Brazil   Chile   Czech Republic   France   Greece
Guatemala   Hungary   Italy   Japan   Poland   Portugal   Singapore
South Korea   Switzerland   Thailand   Turkey   Ukraine   Vietnam

Oxford is a registered trademark of Oxford University Press
in the UK and certain other countries.

Published in the United States of America by
Oxford University Press
198 Madison Avenue, New York, NY 10016

© Oxford University Press 2014

Library of Congress Cataloging-in-Publication Data
Caplan, David, 1969-
Rhyme's challenge : hip hop, poetry, and contemporary rhyming culture /
David Caplan.
pages cm
Includes index.
ISBN 978-0-19-533712-9 (hardcover)—ISBN 978-0-19-533713-6 (pbk.)
1. English language—Rhyme.   2. Hip-hop—United States.   3. American
poetry—20th century—History and criticism.   4. American poetry—21st
century—History and criticism.   I. Title.
PE1517.C36 2014
808.1—dc23
2013030719

9 8 7 6 5 4 3 2 1
Printed in the United States of America
on acid-free paper

CONTENTS

ACKNOWLEDGMENTS

I owe many people many thanks for their help with this book. My students broadened my perspective, offering numerous suggestions, including recommendations of artists whose work I should consider. In particular, I would like to thank Simon Brown for sharing his encyclopedic knowledge of hip hop with me.

Stephen Burt, Adam Bradley, James Longenbach, and Adrian Matejka read the manuscript in its entirety; Heather Dubrow reviewed a chapter. No author could hope for more generous, insightful readers. Even our disagreements proved useful as they challenged me to think harder about rhyme and its many uses.

I have been extremely fortunate to work with talented editors. This project started in a meeting with Shannon McLachlan. Ably assisted by Stephen Bradley, Brendan O'Neill expertly steered the book into publication, with good humor and perceptive guidance. Rick Huard copyedited and arranged permissions.

Several chapters have been presented in various forms at conferences, including the Annual Convention of the Modern Language Association, Arts of the Present Conference, and the Annual Convention of the Association of Writers and Writing Programs, and invited lectures at Bonn University, University of Ghent, and Trinity College, Dublin. I want to thank Ian Kinane, Gillian Groszewski, Stephen Matterson, Frank J. Kearful, Sabine Sielke, Christian Klöckner, and Sarah Posman for arranging these visits and treating me so well during them.

Several fellowships helped me immensely. The Bill and Carol Fox Center for Humanistic Inquiry at Emory University and University of Liège, where I served as a Fulbright Lecturer in American Literature, offered welcoming, stimulating environments. Martine Brownley, Director of the Fox Center, and Michel Delville showed me remarkable hospitality during my time at their respective universities. A Thomas E. Wenzlau Presidential Fellowship from my home institution, Ohio Wesleyan University, gave me time to write. Provosts William Louthan and Charles Stinemetz also deserve thanks for their support.

Finally, this book is dedicated to Ana and Andy.

RHYME'S CHALLENGE

INTRODUCTION

Because It Rhymes

The Gutenberg era, the era of rhyme, is over.
—DONALD DAVIE[1]

that fuddy-duddy device of end-rhyme
—PAUL COLLINS[2]

Most intellectuals will only half-listen.
—NAS[3]

WE LIVE IN A RHYME-DRENCHED era. Rhyme flourishes in advertisements, tabloid headlines, and aphorisms. Nearly all forms of popular music, including country-and-western, rock, pop, punk, soul, and, most notably, hip hop, rhyme. Rhymes fill our lives, crowded with idiosyncratic echoes and associations, both intimate and shared, as rhymes find each other in playgrounds, bedrooms, and on the Internet. The era of rhyme seems over to those who only half-listen. I propose we open our ears and rediscover an amazing rhyming culture.

Consider the following list:

> ta-da Tears for Fears tea tree teeny peeny teeny-weeny teepee

teeter-totter telltale Temporary Contemporary tent
   event
Texas Exes Tex-Mex thigh high think pink thinktank
   thin's in, but fat's where it's at[4]

Harryette Mullen's abecedarian "Jinglejangle" documents
rhymes; it does not invent new ones. It consists of ten pages,
all organized according to alphabetical sequence and rhyme.
The list gives the impression it could continue forever. This
stanza, for instance, ranges widely. It includes erotic arousal
and sexual humiliation, innuendo and insult, fleshly come-
liness ("fat's where it's at"), and emasculating put-down
("teeny-weeny"). It rhymes the thin and the fat, as well as the
adult and juvenile, food and music, the bodily and the intellectual ("thinktank"). Its musical geography encompasses
England, home of the 1980s pop band whose name reportedly truncated the psychologist Arthur Janov's description of
his primal scream method, "tears as a replacement for fears,"[5]
and the American South, where George Strait crooned, "All
my ex's [*sic*] live in Texas/And that's why I hang my hat in
Tennessee."[6] The rhymes recall other rhymes; one example
generates the next. For instance, the Canadian hip-hop artist Drake honors Strait's rhyme, "All my exes live in Texas/
Like I'm George Strait"; Drake carries it across genres as
well as nationalities and races.[7] In this respect, "Jinglejangle"
resembles the website "Pentametron," whose algorithm
charts rhymes that different Twitter user accounts make,
re-tweeting fifteen to twenty couplets daily.[8] When Mullen
read drafts of the poem, she asked the audience for suggestions, some of which she incorporated into later versions.
The poem continues this project; it documents our culture's
propulsive desire to rhyme.

To understand contemporary rhyme, we must listen carefully and widely. Over the course of this book, I will examine legal and political documents, novels, poems, and lyrics from a number of forms of popular music. Together they suggest the technique's far-reaching force and underappreciated sophistication. At a time when expert readers periodically lament poetry's marginality, these examples confirm the great range of rhyming activity at work in our culture.[9] These everyday rhymes demand greater study and less condescension. Accordingly, my analysis seeks to encourage more scholarly work on both neglected texts and the broader underlying issues: for instance, how rhyme functions within and across specific musical and literary genres, not just in individual artists' works, and how it operates in the popular culture, not just in the most prestigious forms of print-based poetry.[10] In this respect, I hope my work might clarify opportunities for future scholarship to pursue.

The most daring, inventive, and conspicuous contemporary rhymers, though, necessarily demand the bulk of my attention. Hip-hop artists dominate the contemporary art of rhyme; they remain most alert to the resources that the culture and the language provide. The effects they achieve are nothing short of astonishing, showing how thrilling rhyme can be, how sexy and appalling. For this reason, most of this book concentrates on their work—more specifically, the kinds of rhymes that hip-hop artists favor: doggerel, insult, and seduction. This attention to particular kinds of rhymes acknowledges both individual and collective achievement, as artists draw from and revise shared techniques. To clarify this accomplishment, I also will review the rhymes' history and current uses. The last chapter will return to the question of hip hop's relation to the most prestigious forms of print-based poetry, considering what a younger generation of American print-based poets has learned from hip hop's achievements.[11]

Hip hop has accomplished so much in rhyme partly because its practitioners hold a particularly useful attitude toward it, one at odds with that of most contemporary print-based poets. This difference extends beyond the striking fact that virtually all hip hop rhymes, even in languages that lack strong traditions of rhyming poetry, whereas the vast majority of contemporary poetry in English does not, even though the language enjoys a strong history of rhyming verse.[12] In this respect, Japan offers an illuminating example. Japanese hip hop, two scholars report, "has come to adopt a notion of rhyme even though there is no basis for it in traditional Japanese poetry."[13] While hip hop defines rhyme as essential to the art, contemporary American poetry and literary criticism typically see rhyme as optional, if not unappealing. Contemporary American print-based poets rarely rhyme and, when they do, they generally do so unobtrusively. They favor less overt rhyming gestures; for instance, they seldom use consistent end rhyme, a visible method of organizing a poem around the technique. The few exceptions—most prominently, Frederick Seidel, the Irish-American Paul Muldoon, and, less consistently, Mullen—almost defiantly depart from the literary norm: to borrow a scholar's description of Muldoon, each might be called "a maverick of rhymes."[14]

Specific attitudes underlie both sets of practices and views. Hip hop possesses a specific confidence in rhyme at odds with American literary culture's general skepticism. Much contemporary poetry criticism repeats a certain truism: in Donald Davie's sweeping phrase, "the era of rhyme" "is over." This idea has grown familiar enough for novelists to parody it.[15] A character in Tobias Wolff's *Old School* rants:

> Rhyme is bullshit. Rhyme says that everything works out in the end. All harmony and order. When I see a rhyme in a poem, I know I'm being lied to. Go ahead, laugh! It's true— rhyme's a completely bankrupt device. It's just wishful thinking. Nostalgia.[16]

Disappointed that his poem did not win the school prize, the schoolboy blames the judge, Robert Frost, a visitor to the prep school, and lashes out at the kind of poetry Frost writes. "I mean, he's still using *rhyme*," the student grumbles, italics underscoring his incredulity and contempt (*OS*, 44). According to this view, rhyme condemns any poet who employs it. It both marks and encourages falsehood. Archaic and morally reprehensible, it perpetuates out-of-date values.[17]

Set in 1960 and published in 2003, *Old School* shows how certain arguments recycle and persist. The novel looks back at an earlier era, while glancing knowingly at the contemporary poetry scene. Such arguments hardly ended in 1960. As if explicating the student's rant, Matthew Zapruder recently declared, "Indeed, nowadays there's simply no way to rhyme and not sound a bit out of time. Our world is too wary and conscious of the different space rhyme and meter create."[18] Zapruder's language remains more measured than the schoolboy's. Both, though, share a similar belief. Rhyme, they insist, cannot escape a particular fate: it always sounds "out of time." It cannot bear the pressure of contemporary reality.

Such assertions are hardly new; in broad terms, they might be called "modernist." Canonical Anglo-American

Modernism did not abandon rhyme; rather, it recrafted the technique. Consider, for instance, the opening lines of T. S. Eliot's "Love Song of J. Alfred Prufrock":

> Let us go then, you and I,
> When the evening is spread out against the sky
> Like a patient etherised upon a table.[19]

In a famous reading, the midcentury American poet John Berryman claimed modern poetry began with the third line. Berryman called the opening couplet "a nice rhyme—it sounds like other dim romantic verse," then noted, "[T]he third line proves that the author of the first two lines did not mean them."[20] In Berryman's language, the author did not mean the opening rhyme or, to be more precise, meant it to convey a jarring force, a diminishment or destruction.[21] This strategy proved immensely influential; it introduced into English what the scholar Daniel Albright calls "a Modernist style of rhyming," "a strain of brittle rhyme." Citing "Prufrock" as well as Ezra Pound's "Hugh Selwyn Mauberley," Albright notes that in such works "rhyming is read as a retreat, a cowering before modern life. In some sense both Prufrock and Mauberley are personifications of rhyme itself, of passé modes of writing poems."[22]

In 1915, such ideas proved groundbreaking; nearly a century later, they inadequately describe a changed state of the art. More recent dismissals of rhyme as old-fashioned and nostalgic face a certain irony; they themselves sound old-fashioned and nostalgic. To add to the confusion, certain recent defenders of rhyme simply reverse the opponents' terms, instead of offering a more precise assessment. "When you rhyme," insists Glyn Maxwell, "you're somehow engaging with something that's older than you are, that's older than your history, that's older than anything you really understand or experience."[23] Mentioned three times in one sentence, rhyme's alleged "oldness" serves as its main virtue.

Directly challenging both sets of assumptions, hip hop dramatically fuses two artistic commitments: rhyme and an intense focus on the contemporary moment. Hip hop is "about what's current," declares Jay-Z, "what's happening right this second."[24] In a characteristic strategy, hip-hop artists rhyme the most conspicuous conditions and symbols of contemporary life: its products, technologies, and personalities. Instead of using rhyme to maintain distance from contemporary culture, hip-hop artists regularly use the technique to evoke the era's distinctive features. Their rhymes couple new inflections, objects of desire, and horrors: rhyming "heaven" with "911" (the Porsche sports car) or "9/11" (the date of the terrorist attack), "Halle Berry" with "very," "Ferrari," or "honorary."[25] The nearly endless effects include the poignant, disconcerting, menacing, charming, attractive, and repellent. Their rhymes name figures of the moment. The odder the name sounds or the more arresting the connection it introduces, the greater its appeal. A master of this technique, Eminem several times offers the grotesque antonym rhyme, "Jeffrey Dahmer" and "Dalai Lama"; he also more lightly couples "naughty rotten rhymer" and "Marty Schottenheimer."[26] In another name-rhyme, Kanye West mixes the ephemeral and the eternal: "The way Kathie Lee needed Regis that's the way I need Jesus."[27] Hip hop's dizzying rush to rhyme the present shows how quickly a cultural moment rushes into the past. West's couplet mentions two talk-show hosts whose names may soon grow as unfamiliar as that of Marty Schottenheimer, a football coach, especially because all three celebrities subsequently retired from the jobs that made them famous. As in the rhyme Mullen records, the "Contemporary" is always "Temporary."

These ambitions inspire a set of rhyming conventions, replete with risks and opportunities. Such procedures depart from familiar models. "In the 'June Book' I made 'breeze' rhyme with 'trees,' and have never forgiven myself," confessed Wallace Stevens. "It is a correct rhyme, of course— but unpardonably 'expected.' "[28] Nearly two centuries earlier, Alexander Pope objected to the same rhyme for the same reason; he ridiculed poets who used "still expected Rhymes":

> Where-e'er you find the cooling Western Breeze,
> In the next Line, it whispers thro' the Trees;
> If Chrystal Streams with pleasing Murmurs creep,
> The Reader's threaten'd (not in vain) with Sleep.[29]

This rhyme persists because it so neatly serves a traditional subject and imagery. Just as nature remains one of lyric poetry's great concerns, the one-syllable rhyme couples two of its stock images, "breeze" and "trees." The rhyme perpetuates a rather bland literary history.

Hip hop's briefer, more frenetic development inspires a different rhyming vocabulary and style. Its artists favor timely references and multisyllabic rhymes as conspicuous as their subjects. Instead of hiding it, they emphasize the competitive nature of artistic technique. To offer the best rhyme is to own the object of desire.

As a demonstration of this principle, luxury cars remain a cliché of hip-hop rhyming. Countless artists, for instance, have rhymed "Lexus." Eye-Ku offers a triple rhyme, "We'll take a spin in a Lexus you can chill for dinner and breakfast/Long enough to see how this gentleman sexes."[30] In an unexceptional hip-hop gesture, the car enhances the speaker's status; it serves as a credential. Through a certain associative logic, the "Lexus" promises that the "breakfast" and the sex will be better. In this respect, the rhyme mimics the effect of countless predecessors, differing only in the specific item named. A greater talent drawing from the same resource, Kanye West rhymes the same car on two songs in one album, each instance playing against this notion of unfettered freedom, sexual and financial. In the first example, a triple rhyme suggests how conspicuous symbols of wealth make their owner into a target: more vulnerable, not more attractive or secure. To underscore this point, the song introduces the thieves before the "necklace" and "Lexus" they desire: "Where restless Niggas might snatch your necklace/And next these Niggas might jack your Lexus."[31] Only three syllables in the two lines do not rhyme or recur. Just as these repetitions choke the couplet, the adjective "restless" menaces the two nouns it rhymes with: "Lexus" and "necklace." The emotion dominates the objects. In the second example, "Lexus" gains a bleaker, ironic meaning; it names a failed aspiration, a pathetic displacement: "Couldn't afford a car so she named her daughter Alexis (a Lexus)."[32] In both examples, West offers a familiar rhyming template but turns the words against their familiar meanings. Instead of preening, the rhymes caution and lament.

Voraciously social, rhyme seeks company. It pursues the new: new couplings, new challenges, new associations. Hip-hop rhymes gain power and force from each other; they achieve canonical status because they have bested other rhymes. Employing the same rhyme as West, "necklace" and "Lexus," the dead prez forcefully recast it. They address the countless hip-hip artists who crow about their cars, asking,

"You would rather have a Lexus? Or justice?/A dream? Or some substance?/A Beamer? A necklace? Or freedom?"[33] The dead prez show how easy it is to rhyme "Lexus" and "necklace"; it is like a nature poet rhyming "breeze" and "trees." To rhyme "Lexus" and "justice," though, is to contrast two competing values and distinguish the artists who espouse them. Anticipating later rhymes such as West's, it introduces a grander artistic ambition.

Like most innovations in art, hip hop's development of rhyme arose through happenstance and cunning. "A DJ gets no damn credit," complained DJ Mister Cee to his collaborator Big Daddy Kane: "Don't look at me funny, Kane cause, yeah, I said it/I'm always in the background." As if unburdening himself, DJ Mister Cee elaborated his grievances with mock fury:

> [A]ll you gotta do is rap.
> Try carrying some console cases on your back.
> Well, I'm through with breaking my neck
> Until you learn to show your DJ some respect.[34]

By 1991, the date of this song's release, the roles of the DJ and MC had grown familiar enough for DJ Mister Cee and Kane to use them for light comedy, to treat each other like they were an affectionately bickering couple. A little more than a decade before, this banter would have made little sense; a role reversal had transformed the art. In the late 1970s, S. Craig Watkins recalls, "rap music" "was essentially a live performance-art form that complemented the hip hop's main attraction, the DJ":

> Ironically, some DJs began to rhyme or add MCs as a way to keep rivals from stealing their two most prized

possessions: their records and their technique. In just a few short years, though, the roles reversed, with MCs becoming the main attraction and DJs serving in many instances as background accompaniment.[35]

Attuned to shifting artistic values and opportunities, the performers reinvented their art, alert to how contemporary language functions, how words can be twisted, combined, and recast. A DJ who wanted respect took the microphone and rhymed. The background claimed the fore.

At first, the form's very idea proved inspirational. Wistfully looking back at the early 1980s, Speech from Arrested Development recalled how these early hip-hop artists enjoyed a certain benefit:

> The rhyme styles is more simple from back in the day to some extent, but it was because it was so fresh—the whole thing was just fresh, the whole idea. MCs today [are] adding on to what's already there, whereas cats back in the day, they really was creating something from scratch—the foundation hadn't been laid as much.[36]

As Speech's comments suggest, this moment of "creating something from scratch" did not last long. With a ruthless, competitive drive, the quickly established art demanded innovation: new styles and revisions, new rhymes.

Other movements fed off these developments while resisting some of their features. Slam poetry arose from different circumstances than hip hop: starting in the mid-1980s, it grew from contests held in white working-class bars in Chicago. Like many practitioners, though, techniques moved from one art form to the other. Slam poetry's "formal characteristics," Susan B. A. Somers-Willett relates, "often reflect the influence of hip-hop; indeed, regularly rhymed poetry is usually recognized by poets and audience members as extensions of a hip-hop tradition not as formalist poetry."[37] At the same time, some slam poets utilize rhyme to express their reservations about hip-hop culture and values. In this context, to use the technique differently is to espouse a different politics. "Hip-hop has failed its mission," declares Guy LeCharles Gonzalez, the 1998 National Poetry Slam Champion, distinguishing between "slam poets" and "wannabe rap stars": "I'm tired of seeing the revolution compromised/by wannabe rap stars disguised as slam poets." Later in the same poem Gonzalez elaborates on the distinction: "You're not a poet/you just slam a lot//cram a lot of senseless rhyming."[38] The lines bear hip hop's inspiration yet turn against it. As the first couplet suggests, more elaborate rhyme—that is, the kind hip hop favors—offers a form of political "compromise" and "disguise." Accordingly, the slam poet faces a choice between "the revolution" and "senseless rhyming": in broad terms, between good politics and bad aesthetics. Signaling his commitments, the slam poem uses rhyme less frequently than hip-hop songs typically do, as if holding the technique in check. Tempered and sober, the rhyme "slam"/"cram" also reinforces the poet's assertion that he pursues the first option, that he stays uncompromised: socially responsible and devoted to the proper goals. According to the poem, the right rhyming style advances "the revolution," although, of course, the poem never reveals exactly how. Instead, the poet's formal gestures most powerfully express his aspirations and artistic debts, and record how intertwined they remain.

"The debates over popular art," the philosopher Richard Shusterman notices, rarely leave "the familiar poles of condemnatory pessimism and celebratory optimism."[39] In the case of hip hop, these debates came in two stages. In the first, the optimists tended to praise the artists for their truth-telling, calling them "prophets of the hood" and rap "the black CNN" (in Chuck D's often-quoted metaphor).[40] The pessimists typically criticized the music for a perceived detrimental social influence, for the promotion of misogyny, consumerism, and violence, or for the inaccurate representations of cultural conditions, for "keepin' it unreal" (in Ta-Nehisi Coates's term).[41] Both the optimists and pessimists focused on how the "stories" that hip-hop artists "tell" "articulate" sociopolitical realities.[42] The critical terms often remained ideological, even when the music was discussed as "art." For this reason, the first generation of hip-hop scholarship favored cultural histories and criticism. Such modes of analysis rarely show detailed interest in poetic form and versification. When praising a rhyme's quality, many critics simply quote the passage, as if the fact that the words rhyme proves the performer's virtuosity.

In the last few years, the terms of the debate have shifted. Given the culture's general indifference to poetics, the question of whether hip hop should be considered poetry generates a surprisingly intense debate. In *Book of Rhymes: The Poetics of Hip Hop*, Adam Bradley, the most sophisticated defender of hip hop as poetry, asserts, "Rap is poetry," slyly adding, "but its popularity relies in part on people not recognizing it as such."[43] *The Anthology of Rap,* which Bradley coedited with Andrew DuBois, documents the claim. The anthology quickly announces its goal; it "tells the story of rap as lyric poetry."[44] Suggesting a widespread interest in this argument, literary journals that typically ignore popular music reviewed the anthology. Even the attacks suggest it could not be ignored. In both books, Bradley responded to a specific history of condescension and ignorance. His arguments for hip hop as poetry invert the usual terms of artistic censure. Mark Strand, for example, sweepingly maintained, "There's no connection between rap and poetry.... I can't listen to it. It's like being blasted up against a wall."[45] A small anthology might record similar pronouncements from distinguished poets, critics, and anthologists. To dismiss hip hop as "poetry" on these terms, then, is to dismiss it as unworthy of attention.[46]

Such arguments about hip hop as "poetry" might attend more closely to two complications. First, too often critics treat the term "poetry" as if it retains a stable definition across cultures, time periods, and genres. The history of poetics, however, records much more contestation than consensus. With particular vehemence modern and contemporary poets gleefully turn against the most popular definitions. They form targets, not touchstones. In his "Preface" to *Lyrical Ballads*, William Wordsworth offered a classic definition: "[P]oetry is the spontaneous overflow of powerful feelings: it takes its origin from emotion recollected in tranquillity" (*CW*, 292). Taking aim at the second half of the sentence, T. S. Eliot rejected nearly every word, calling it "an inexact formula. For it is neither emotion, nor recollection, nor without distortion of meaning, tranquillity."[47] Playing his own variations on Wordsworth's words, Charles Bernstein revises the heartfelt declaration into a line of nonsense verse: "Poetry is tranquillity recollected in emotion, commotion projected in tranquillity, recollection unsettled by turbulence."[48] A poet temperamentally different from both Bernstein and Eliot, Thom Gunn also turns Wordsworth's words against him. Instead of clinically dismembering Wordsworth's phrases, Gunn recasts them into a sordid, mocking rhyme, "*Spontaneous overflows of powerful feeling:*/Wet dreams, wet dreams, in libraries congealing."[49] "Close up those barren leaves," advises Wordsworth in a phrase that Gunn pointedly borrows for his couplet's title.[50] In the history of poetics, poets often regard others' definitions of the art similarly: as fruitless and dead.

Second, the debates about hip hop as poetry overlook an important possibility. The current debate largely focuses on issues of cultural prestige. Accordingly, it often defines poetry as an honorific term. To call hip hop "poetry" is to raise its cultural standing; to reject it as "poetry" is to deny it a certain status. Hip hop, however, contributes most to the fields of poetry and poetics once we acknowledge that it differs significantly from the most prestigious forms of contemporary poetry. The distinctions prove to be the most valuable. Even when the two forms approach each other, they do so from opposing positions and according to opposite trajectories. Despite the development of other kinds of poetry, including those that use verbal performance or the resources of the web, the most prestigious forms of contemporary poetry largely remain print-based. It is a commonplace of contemporary poetry criticism and pedagogy that to be experienced fully, print-based poetry must be read aloud. "If we can read it silently," Jorge Luis Borges declared, "it is not a valid poem: a poem demands pronunciation."[51] For this reason, many teachers of poetry insist that their students read the assigned poems aloud and many textbooks present this technique as a necessity. A certain kind of hip-hop lyric, though, demands nearly the opposite progression. Crafted according to the demands of musical performance, it seeks to be transcribed and considered as a silent written text. Responding to this call, students of hip hop construct numerous website databases that catalogue thousands of lyrics, so viewers can study them as words set into stanzas. "Do you fools listen to music or do you just skim through it?"[52] asks Jay-Z. To "listen to music" intelligently, then, is to write it down, to read it attentively. Encouraging this process, many hip-hop artists welcome archival efforts to document and analyze their work, recognizing that this study validates their artistry. Nas, for instance, contributes to the "Rap Genius" website while Jay-Z published a book, complete with his own annotations, to help listeners "decode that torrent of words."[53]

Studied in this way, hip hop challenges the most prestigious forms of contemporary poetry. It does not do so by establishing another commonly accepted definition of "poetry." The definitions that artists propose vary, even when those involved share the desire to claim this title for their art. A certain irony arises from this situation. If, to certain hip-hop artists, the presence of rhyme establishes the work as "poetry," it also distinguishes it from the most prestigious forms of contemporary poetry. "Hip Hop is poetry. All Hip Hop is poetry. It rhymes," asserts Mos Def, offering a definition that highlights the contrast.[54] In this respect, rhyme marks a difference, not a similarity.

A different sense of the language reinforces this distinction. Literary critics often report that English contains relatively few rhymes and that this scarcity makes English hostile to the technique. "Of the Indo-Germanic languages," John Bayley maintains, "English is probably the most recalcitrant in matters of rhyme."[55] According to this logic, rhyme's paucity or abundance inevitably inspires a certain effect. "[I]n a rime-haunted language like Provençal or Italian," observed Leslie Fiedler, "a poem which rejects rime" "seems not a relaxation but an effort of the will."[56] In English, the terms apparently reverse. "Why rhyme?" John Hollander asks before answering, "To make it harder."[57] According to this logic, rhymes in English defy the language's given features. They organize the poem around a relatively meager resource.

Hip-hop rhymes give a very different impression of the language and the ease, willfulness, and difficulty of rhyming. Instead of resisting the language's given features, they reveal a propulsive drive toward rhyme at work in the culture, a nearly boundless resource. Doggerel presents the most striking example, but the other kinds of rhyming I will discuss also dramatize that basic drive: language's need to couple. Seduction rhymes exploit this dynamic when they embody desire by pairing sounds. In them, we hear the carnality of rhyme. With a crueler intent, insult rhymes use a sonic coincidence as if the language itself proved the association. "The most potent of counterlogical devices," Frank Kermode notes, "is rhyme."[58] Exploiting this fact, insult rhyme uses the technique to align logic and counterlogic, as if the language itself were revealing an undeniable truth.

In profound and trivial ways, rhyme abounds. As if to document this point, when Zapruder dismisses the technique as unworthy of the contemporary moment, his denunciation rhymes: "there's simply no way to *rhyme*/and not sound a bit out of *time*" (my italics). Rhyme is bipartisan and nearly inescapable; it elevates and debases those who employ it. During the 2008 presidential elections, Republican crowds chanted, "Vote McCain, Not Hussein." Asked by a reporter to explain, one of the chant's leaders responded, "Because it rhymes."[59] The technique offered a justification and an excuse. It both disavowed the crowd's responsibility for the argument it made and served as evidence. It helped the slander sound true, at least to those inclined to believe it. A rhyme can work even more efficiently; it can consist of a single syllable. During the campaign a portrait of the Republican vice-presidential nominee Sarah Palin circulated on the Internet.[60] In color and style, it evoked Shepard Fairey's iconic image of Barack Obama. Labeled "NOPE," instead of "HOPE," the poster encouraged the viewer to think of other rhyming insults to add, to think "dope," "mope," and so on. It gave a structure to an instinct: that Palin deserved nearly any abuse the viewer could add. Rhymes, though, transcend any individual's control. A few years into the Obama presidency *The Advocate* featured a similar image titled, "Nope?" with a subtitle: "He was our greatest hope, but he has yet to deliver."[61] The same rhyme reworks a welcomed promise into an accusation.

Rhyme, then, conveys danger as well as promise. Its use involves certain risks. It can inspire mistakes, minor or grave. It can mislead. A poem by D. A. Powell ends with "an excess of bubkes might please."[62] An endnote glosses the line: " 'bubkes': a Yiddish word that means both 'nothing' and 'potato pancakes' " (*T*, 70). The note is half right; bubkes is "a Yiddish word which means" " 'nothing.' " In Yiddish, "potato pancakes," though, are "latkes," not "bubkes." It seems plausible to assume that a rhyme of "bubkes" and "latkes" facilitated the slip, persuading the poet that the two words were one.

More serious is the case of Professor Tyrone Hayes. Hayes swiftly achieved impressive success as an academic. Educated at Harvard and the University of California, Berkeley, and the recipient of many grants and awards for his research and teaching, he quickly earned tenure at Berkeley and, three years later, promotion to full professorship at the age of thirty-five. A world-class biology researcher specializing in amphibian endocrinology, Hayes studies how exposure to certain chemicals affects frogs and, by implication, the animal and human ecosystem. In the late 1990s, he and his research team conducted an experiment in which the results revealed that exposure to atrazine, the world's most common herbicide, causes male frogs to exhibit female characteristics and to develop a number of other reproductive deformities and conditions, including retarded gonadal development, testicular oogenesis, gonadal dysgenesis, and hermaphroditism.[63] Hayes and the other members of his team subsequently published more than a dozen widely noticed articles on the subject in peer-reviewed journals, drawing considerable attention to the issue. The initial article, for instance, received over seven hundred citations. As he continued his research, its implications grew more disturbing. Hayes claimed that exposure to atrazine also increases the risks for cancer in humans.

To advocate for what he saw as the public good, Hayes gave numerous talks to scholarly and lay audiences, warning them of atrazine's allegedly deleterious effects. With a charming, affable style, he occasionally delivered a rhyming call to action, punctuated by the audience's delighted applause and laughter:

> So let me remind you, don't put this behind you:
> atrazine ain't a good thing.
> It causes male frogs to grow eggs,
> contributes to extra legs,
> and exposed males don't want to sing.[64]

Faced with a skilled, charismatic, and determined critic, Syngenta Crop Protection, the maker of atrazine, responded by contesting Hayes's research methods and conclusions and by funding alternative studies. They also sent representatives to Hayes's talks in order to defend the product, a major component of its selective herbicide line, which earned $2.3 billion in just one year. Asked by a reporter, a spokeswoman explained, "A Syngenta representative does try to attend events where Dr. Hayes is speaking.... It's in our best interest, and farmers', that we have the opportunity to counter his outrageous accusations."[65]

In 2010, Syngenta also submitted a formal ethics complaint against Hayes to his employer, the University of California, Berkeley, complaining of "aggressive, unprofessional, and insulting," "salacious and lewd" emails directed to company employees. As part of the complaint, the company submitted what it called a "barrage of emails," making more than eighty examples public.[66] It is unclear what particular grievance inspired Hayes's emails. Several allude to an intensely personal feud that apparently developed between Hayes and a company employee who shadowed him at his speaking engagements. (In interviews, Hayes alleged persistent harassment.) The emails make strange, disorienting reading. Quotations from hip-hop artists abound, including passages from songs by Tupac Shakur, DMX, and Public Enemy, as well as Hayes's own battle rhymes, sometimes modeled on these influences. Frequently the emails quote hip-hop slogans. "[H]ip hop don't stop baby!" one exclaims as if enlisting the music to his cause.[67] Hayes's own verses taunt, threaten, and boast:

> tyrone b hayes is hard as h*ll
> battle anybody, i don't care who you tell!
> you object! you will fail!
> mercy for the weak is not for sale![68]

Hayes's lines recast the famous opening of LL Cool J's "Rock the Bells," with a few evocative changes:

> LL Cool J is hard as hell.
> Battle anybody I don't care who you tell.
> I excel, they all fail.
> I'm gonna crack shells, Double-L must rock the bells.[69]

In addition to rhyme, Hayes borrows the song's grammatical form. Like LL Cool J, Hayes refers to himself in the grander third person, but Hayes substitutes his name in place of the nicknames the hip-hop performer employed. As if insisting on the power and the respect that the fuller name conveys, Hayes also introduces his middle initial, recasting "tyrone b hayes" into a hip-hop moniker. A mixture of bouts-rimés and quotation, the final line replaces LL Cool J's slangy hook with a multilevel threat, "mercy for the weak is not for sale." To brag about his integrity, Hayes reworks this moral quality into the form of a battle rhyme. He does not appeal for "mercy" since that strategy would assign him the role of the weaker party. Instead of morality, he presents a contest of masculinity. Faced with Hayes's virility, the multinational, billion-dollar corporation cannot compete with his self-professed hardness.

Labeled "Exhibit A" in the complaint, a single rhyming quatrain recasts this claim into blunt, scatological language and imagery:

> aww shucks...I'm bouta' handle my biz right now
> see you bucked...wondering... "what it is right now?"
> ya outa' luck...bouta show you how it is right now
> see you're ****ed (i didn't pull out) and ya fulla my j*z
>   right now![70]

This quatrain follows an intricate rhyming pattern familiar to hip hop. The lines open with a four-group rhyme group and end with a repeated phrase preceded by another four-group rhyme. Both rhymes build to an expletive, its letters replaced with asterisks like a word bleeped by a radio censor. The concluding repeated phrase, "right now," adds menace, insisting on the threat's imminence.

It is difficult to define precisely the role that rhyme played in these incidents. If academic conferences exist to publicize both the research and the researcher, the rhymes Hayes performed at his talks masterfully accomplished both goals. When his rhymes switched genres from uplifting "message" hip hop to hardcore battle rhymes, the change introduced another, nearly disastrous set of conventions. As in hip-hop beefs, Hayes personalized all disagreement and sought to exploit any perceived weakness. The genre encouraged a certain language and style, the expression of particular attitudes. Rhyme and its techniques gave the structure to a desire, perhaps even a fantasy, helping Hayes see parallels between his work as a scientist and that of a battle rhymer. Once, as if realizing the difference, he almost touchingly asks, "[C]an you believe that someone wants to publish my emails and rhymes? like some kind of book of poetry?"[71]

Not surprisingly, Syngenta used these emails to discredit Hayes and question his credibility, releasing the messages with the company's complaint and publicizing them. The Internet filled with both the emails and the discussion of them. Titled "The Strange Case of Dr. Tyrone Hayes," a blog on the *Atrazine News* website darkly claimed, "Now we have evidence that Dr. Hayes is not only biased but seriously unbalanced in his attitude toward atrazine and its manufacturer, Syngenta."[72] Another industry blog observed, "Self-proclaimed anti-atrazine activist researcher damages his already shaky cred with e-mails."[73] Given the gravity of the situation, this charge carries significant financial, legal, and ecological consequences. Potentially it affects public health policy as well as litigation. For instance, Syngenta settled one lawsuit for $105 million.[74] At the very least, Hayes's emails distract attention from the grave dangers he believes the widely used herbicide poses.

As this example suggests, rhyme retains the potential to threaten those who use it. It proves irresistible, even when inappropriate. Unlike his peer-reviewed scientific research written in the technical, scholarly style suitable to it, Hayes's rhymes remain highly quotable to a nonspecialist audience. Outrageous, they are hard to forget. Once made public, this memorability turned into a vulnerability. They made the distinguished biologist easy to mock.

"[H]ow could anyone be hurt by a mere rhyme?" Paul de Man once asked.[75] Rhyme crosses private and public spheres, animating insults and personal ruminations. Seizing upon its wide circulation and cultural force, hip hop commits to the technique in ways that literary criticism finds hard to take seriously, let alone understand. Hip-hop artists see the technique as powerful, not ineffectual. They injure, as well as seduce and charm. I have titled this book *Rhyme's Challenge* because hip hop usefully challenges a host of entrenched positions in contemporary poetry, poetry criticism, and poetics. With particular intensity, their accomplishments challenge the notion of rhyme as old fashioned. Committed to the technique, hip-hop artists reclaim certain effects from the longer history of English-language verse, which the most prestigious forms of print-based poetry have largely discarded. In this respect, they challenge prevalent notions of "poetry" by showing how much they exclude. They also remind attentive listeners how innovation works: how it mixes historical reclamation and contemporary discoveries until they become nearly indistinguishable. If, in certain respects, hip-hop artists are more "traditional" than many print-based poets, they also remain keenly alert to the contemporary moment. Resisted and admired, their rhymes record a lover's quarrel with the most prestigious forms of contemporary poetry. So does this book.

REDUCED TO RHYME

Contemporary Doggerel

IN SEPTEMBER 2001, THE SUPREME Court of Pennsylvania ruled that Susan Porreco could not void her prenuptial agreement because she had received a cubic zirconium engagement ring. When she met her future husband, Susan Porreco was a seventeen-year-old high school student living with her parents; he was a forty-five-year-old, previously married millionaire and the owner of a car dealership. After two years of dating, he proposed, presenting her with a ring that she claimed he said was a diamond. Though Louis Porreco later insisted that he did not mislead his fiancée about the stone, he listed the ring's value as $21,000 on the prenuptial agreement that his lawyer drafted. When the couple separated after ten years of marriage, she hired a jeweler to appraise the ring. Her lawsuit sought to dissolve the prenuptial agreement based on the misrepresentation.[1]

The court found for Louis Porreco, maintaining that his ex-wife should have obtained "an appraisal of the ring" when it was first given to her and faulting her "failure to do this simple investigation." In a dissenting opinion, Justice Michael Eakin asserted:

> A groom must expect matrimonial pandemonium
> When his spouse finds he's given her a cubic zirconium
> Instead of a diamond in her engagement band,
> The one he said was worth twenty-one grand. (*PP*, 575–576)

Addressing the legal standard of "fraudulent misrepresentation," which requires "justifiable reliance on the misrepresentation," Justice Eakin continued in rhyming couplets:

> Given their history and Pygmalion relation,
> I find her reliance was with justification.
> Given his accomplishment and given her youth,
> Was it unjustifiable for her to think he told the truth?
> Or for every prenuptial, is it now a must
> That you treat your betrothed with presumptive mistrust?
> Do we mean reliance on your beloved's representation
> Is not justifiable, absent third party verification?
> Love, not suspicion, is the underlying foundation
> Of parties entering the marital relation. (*PP*, 576)

Justice Eakin's opinion distressed his colleagues. In concurring opinions, two of his fellow justices objected specifically to his use of rhyme. Chief Justice Stephen Zappala wrote of his "grave concern that the filing of an opinion that expresses itself in rhyme reflects poorly on the Supreme Court of Pennsylvania" (*PP*, 572). The Chief Justice protested on two grounds. First, rhyme diverts attention from the court's true concerns: "[I]t is the substance of our views that should be the focus of our discussion" (572). For this reason, rhyme's excessive stylization presents a distraction. Second and more disturbingly, its use in a legal document undermines the court's authority. "The dignity of the Supreme Court of Pennsylvania," Chief Justice Zappala insisted, "should not be diminished" (572). Rhyme, he fears, trivializes the proceedings. The loss of "dignity" endangers the court as an institution because it reduces its credibility and effectiveness. Rhyme encourages the public to see the court itself as frivolous. Agreeing with the Chief Justice, Justice Ralph Cappy focused on the second line of argument: "My concern… and the point on which I concur completely with the Chief Justice, lies with the perception that litigants and the public at large might form when an opinion of the Court is reduced to rhyme" (572).

Justice Cappy's phrase, "reduced to rhyme," nicely captures the technique's present status. "Rhyme these days is in bad repute," notes Hugh Kenner.[2] Rhymes abound in contemporary culture yet we devalue the technique's significance. Outside of certain occasions, rhymes' persistent claims feel awkward. As First Lady, Hillary Clinton often recalled a favorite quatrain:

> As I was standing in the street
> As quiet as could be
> A great big ugly man came up
> And tied his horse to me[3]

As with Clinton, rhymes can enter our thoughts, seemingly of their own volition. Repeated aloud, they sound unsavory, if not embarrassing.

A certain history complicates this situation. Contemporary songs rhyme to a much greater degree than do poems, a tendency that reverses the basic trajectory of English poetry. As the literature developed, poets parted ways with Greek and Latin authors who typically wrote unrhymed verse composed to be sung. Written to be spoken or read on the page, poetry in English broke with classical tradition by rhyming. In Renaissance debates about versification, rhyme represented a modern technique, regardless of whether the participant decried rhyme as a "troublesome and modern bondage" or celebrated it as the "the chief life" of "modern" "versifying."[4] By the eighteenth century, many observers had declared the argument settled. "[R]hyming is what I have ever accounted the very essential of a good poet," Jonathan Swift advised a younger poet, adding, "And in that notion I am not singular." To illustrate this lesson, Swift labored to develop an adequate metaphor for rhyme's extensive powers. "Verse without rhyme is a body without a soul," he wrote, "or a bell without a clapper."[5] Many poets and critics similarly maintained that rhyme defined the language's poetry. "Rhyme," Swinburne affirmed in 1867, building to his own comparison, "is the native condition of lyric verse in English: a rhymeless lyric is a maimed thing."[6] No knowledgeable reader of poetry holds this position today.

A change in translation marks this historical shift. Many Renaissance and eighteenth-century translators cast unrhymed classical verse into rhyming couplets; those who did not protested the dominant mode. "It is commonly said that rhyme is to be abandoned in a translation of Homer," Matthew Arnold observed.[7] It seems odd to maintain that a translator of Homer who does not use rhyme has "abandoned" the technique, because the original does not rhyme. Instead, Arnold's point makes sense in a specific context. A translator who does not rhyme has "abandoned" the techniques familiar to the English verse tradition. Though Arnold objects to rhymed translations, his telling verb suggests the technique's lingering influence at the time. A different assumption characterizes the contemporary era. Many contemporary translators employ the opposite procedures from Dryden, Pope, and Chapman. Instead of adding rhymes to blank verse, they translate rhyming verse without rhymes. They remove the element, instead of adding it. Asked about translating Borges into English, Norman Thomas di Giovanni minces few words: "Rhyme is hardly poetry, and we found it quite expendable."[8] Pithily, Di Giovanni renounces any regret. With a superlative and an intensifier, he characterizes rhyme as irrelevant to the work's artistry and unnecessary: "hardly poetry" and "quite expendable." Other translators cite pragmatic reasons, involving the difficulties that rhyme poses. "This is doing it the easy way," Robert Hass self-deprecatingly explains, "which has been typical of late twentieth century translation. I ignored the rhymes."[9] This decision signals the value that translators place on the technique; it presents a problem they need not address.

Regarding the contemporary scene, many literary critics view patterned rhyme as frivolous and beside the point, a distraction. Referring to "our rhyme-resistant time," J. Paul Hunter notes how even sophisticated contemporary readers struggle to understand the complexity of rhyming verse: "It hardly seems possible, in our rhyme-resistant time, to take the couplet or its contents seriously except as repression—even to avid historical readers and professional critics."[10] A scholar of eighteenth-century literature, Hunter recognizes that this prejudice obscures a major historic form. "[C]ouplets," he notes, "dominated all poetry" "for more than two hundred years, nearly half the recognizable English tradition" ("SB," 2). As if to confirm Hunter's fears, Marjorie Perloff returns to the same example, untroubled by the situation that Hunter laments. Perloff claims that "today, the very appearance of heroic couplets" "is a signifier of "light verse," something fun and parodic, not meant to be taken too seriously."[11] In her first book, *Rhyme and Meaning in the Poetry of Yeats*, Perloff explored the variety of effects that rhyme offers a single great poet.[12] Four decades later, Perloff implies that contemporary poets who write noncomic heroic couplets commit a mistake because the form serves as "a signifier of 'light verse.'" It no longer evokes the wider range of genres, including the heroic, dramatic, and amorous modes that previous masters of the couplet have explored. In such arguments, the heroic couplet, the clearest major rhyme scheme, serves as a metonymy for all rhyming poetry; such assertions reduce endstopped rhyme to an essentially comic technique, not a flexible medium capable of expressing a range of attitudes, ideas, and emotions.

But what about noncomic rhyming verse, poetry "meant to be taken seriously"? Lyn Hejinian explains why the presence of rhyme dooms such efforts:

> An English poem in a regular meter and with its lines hammered into position by end-rhymes tends to have a tiresome though sometimes laughable predictability; at best, it suggests only ancient wisdom, age-old truths. It provides familiarity and, through familiarity, consolation. It gives us respite from the hardships of life.[13]

Hejinian believes that end rhymes in English make poetry "laughable," regardless of the effect the writer wishes to achieve. If the author aims to express moral seriousness, rhyme allows only bombast. The technique decides the result, condemning the poetry to "familiarity and, through familiarity, consolation," all of which Hejinian sees as undesirable. According to her, all rhyming poems remain essentially the same, whether written in forms as different as the ghazal, the ballad, and villanelle or by poets of varying artistic temperaments.

Such sweeping dismissals ignore the details of actual practice. Justice Eakin, for instance, favors a specific kind of rhyme. "A rhyme must have in it some slight element of surprise if it is to give pleasure," Ezra Pound asserted. "[I]t need not be bizarre or curious, but it must be well used if used at all."[14] Pound's Imagist dictum has achieved the status of a truism, cited in nearly all discussions of the technique. At his most compelling, though, Eakin works from the opposite principle. When his line "A groom must expect matrimonial pandemonium" sets "pandemonium" as the opening element in the rhyme pair, an attentive reader familiar with the case awaits "zirconium." At least two factors draw the reader to this conclusion. Few rhymes exist for "pandemonium"; *Merriam-Webster's Rhyming Dictionary*, for instance, lists only four.[15] Within such a narrow range of options, "cubic zirconium" remains a conspicuous possibility, especially because the fake jewel represents a memorable symbol of deceit, the one detail all acquainted with the case will remember. Tacky as the ring it describes, the rhyme confirms the reader's suspicion; it delights as much in its own bad taste as in the bad taste it reports. Instead of building to a surprise, it confirms the reader's expectations. The rhyme gives the pleasure of an unsuppressed groan.

Another bit of legal verse clarifies Eakin's method. In her decision in a 1989 case before the United States Supreme Court, Justice Sandra Day O'Connor cited Shakespeare's lines, "But I'll amerce you with so strong a fine/That you shall all repent the loss of mine," in order to document a historical meaning of "fine."[16] Writing for the majority, Justice Harry Blackmun retorted with his own verse:

> Though Shakespeare, of course,
> Knew the Law of his time,
> He was foremost a poet,
> In search of a rhyme. (*BF*, 266, n. 7)

Justice Blackmun's rhyme against rhyme embodies the point it makes. It presents rhyme as an easy trick that gives invention the appearance of truth. Rhyme, it suggests, performs two functions. The technique introduces a potential falsification, as words are chosen less for their meaning than for their sounds. The presence of rhyme discredits Shakespeare's words; it diminishes their evidentiary value, because Shakespeare "was foremost a poet/In search of a rhyme." The technique also achieves a second, seemingly incompatible effect. Rhyme gives Justice Blackmun's stanza an air of certitude; "time" and "rhyme" cinch his argument with a certain rhetorical authority. The justice, then, exploits the very technique whose credibility he seeks to undermine.

Blackmun and Eakin write doggerel, the rhyming form that suffers the lowest standing. Often the term doubles as a pejorative, referring to bad or inept poetry. "Tastes shift," a literary historian states, "and what looks to one generation like 'major poetry' often reads like doggerel to the next."[17] "Major poetry" and "doggerel" represent antonyms, marking literature's extremes. Like the term's etymology, the genre itself seems "poor, worthless."[18] A kind of verse to be shunned, not appreciated, doggerel has enjoyed little critical attention.

In two notable exceptions, George Saintsbury and Northrop Frye attempted to understand its origins and distinguish its types. Both attempt to extricate a genre from its disagreeable manifestations; they explore (in Saintsbury's analogy) "a subject as inseparably connected with prosody as vice is with virtue."[19] Each, then, splits doggerel into two types: "doggerel which is doggerel, and doggerel which is not." According to Saintsbury, the former is "merely bad verse— verse which attempts a certain form or norm, and fails" (*HEP*, 392). When discussing the "good" kind, Saintsbury stresses its rarity and the enormous demands it places on the poet. "[I]t would require," he writes, "a Dantean ingenuity and an ultra-Dantean good-nature to niche it in Paradise" (*HEP*, 393). The "doggerel which is not" features a recognizable verse form and poetic language "with a wilful licentiousness which is excused by the felicitous result" (393). Such poetry violates decorum by employing verse's conventional markers. It registers "a direct though perhaps unconscious *protest* against the inadequacy, against the positive faultiness, of the regular prosody of the time" (394). Saintsbury italicizes "protest" as if to disguise the two words that modify it. Only two paragraphs before, Saintsbury stresses that the good kind of doggerel requires conscious effort: "The poet is not trying to do what he cannot do; he is trying to do something exceptional, outrageous, shocking—and does it to admiration" (393). As the sentence moves from a negative to a positive assertion, Saintsbury insists that the poet achieves his goal; he accomplishes what he "is trying to do." This success distinguishes good doggerel from bad, which simply fails the "form" or "norm" it attempts. The hedging phrase, "perhaps unconscious *protest*," introduces the suggestion that the protest it registers might not be wholly deliberate. The modifier leaves open the possibility that "perhaps" the poem's force derives from other sources.

Frye more confidently returns to this issue, although he does not cite Saintsbury's work. As the terms Frye introduces make clear, "intention" distinguishes real doggerel from intentional doggerel. For Frye, the versions share two similarities; they retain an underlying prose rhythm and "the features of rhyme and meter become grotesque."[20] Doggerel does not fully develop from prose into poetry; it perversely uses the visible features of verse. What distinguishes "intentional" doggerel from "real" doggerel is that a greater self-consciousness inspires the better kind, as its author knowingly utilizes the devices that naïve writers automatically use. For this reason, the writers of "intentional" "doggerel" oppose the writers of "real" "doggerel." The more sophisticated doggerel poets turn against the others, making them objects of ridicule. "What makes intentional doggerel funny," Frye observes,

> is its implied parody of real doggerel, or incompetent attempts at verse: the struggle for rhymes, even to the mispronouncing of words, the dragging in of ideas for the sake of a rhyme, the distorting of syntax in squeezing words into meter. (*WTC*, 70)

"Intentional doggerel" feasts on its unaccomplished twin, recasting the same grotesque techniques. In particular, shrewder doggerel poets such as Byron and Browning exploit a generic quirk. In parody and in satire, doggerel's vices turn into virtues, an effect Frye celebrates, declaring, "[D]oggerel in satire is a sign of wit rather than incompetence."[21]

In Frye's terms, both Justice O'Connor and Justice Blackmun write "intentional doggerel." An example of anti-poetry, Blackmun's quatrain mocks poetry as a means of knowledge. Instead of parodying "incompetent attempts at verse," he addresses Shakespeare, the language's most celebrated poet. As if to invoke his predecessor, Blackmun uses the same rhyme group centuries later, turning Shakespeare's sounds against him. To discredit O'Connor's evidence, Blackmun places the law above poetry, presenting a judge's words as truer than the poet's. Eakin's verse rhymes legal terminology ("representation," "third party verification," "underlying foundation," and "marital relation") as well as some of the case's more salacious details. The verse juxtaposes the law's august abstractions and the case's seedier reality. In a reversal of Frye's aesthetic standard, this "intentional doggerel" strikes me as more objectionable in a legal context. The verse techniques register a certain attitude toward the litigants and their plight; it casts them as the subjects of light comedy. In a sense, the poetry's departure from artistic decorum parallels its departure from legal decorum. In blunt terms, Eakin writes his opinion in doggerel because he finds the case funny.[22]

The two poems provide fairly clear examples of a murky genre in which "intentional" and "real doggerel" are not so easily distinguished. As Saintsbury's hedge suggests, a rhyme precariously marks what the author "is trying to do." Composition blurs the accidental and the intentional; a rhyme introduces unexpected opportunities based in sonic coincidences. "[T]he chain reaction of a rhyme," relates Seamus Heaney, "can proceed happily and as it were autistically, in an area of mental operations cordoned off by and from the critical sense."[23] Following Pound, many poets report that rhymes "surprise" and "astonish" them, divert-ing the emerging poems from their original intentions.[24] Depending on their temperaments, critics and poets have proposed spiritual metaphors for this process or described it as inscrutable.[25] W. H. Auden drew from philosophy to define the composition process as dialectical:

> In the process of composition, as every poet knows, the rela-tion between experience and language is always dialectical, but in the finished product it must always appear to the reader to be a one-way relationship. In serious poetry thought, emotion, event, must always appear to dictate the diction, meter, and rhyme in which they are embodied; vice versa, in comic poetry it is the words, meter, rhyme, which must appear to create the thoughts emotions, and events they require.[26]

Shrewdly Auden distinguishes between the actual process of composition and the appearance the poem gives. A master of the two modes he mentions, Auden realizes that poets cultivate their readers' confidence. To do so, they establish command of their art, albeit in different ways. Depending on the kind of verse they compose, they project mastery or feign incompetence. Each mode requires an appropriate appearance.

Hip hop, though, does not respect such sensible distinc-tions between "intentional" and "real" doggerel, or comic and serious poetry. Instead of renouncing rhyme, hip hop com-mits fully and openly to it. Again and again, the art reveals the technique's flexibility. A single hip-hop song may con-tain astonishingly different kinds of rhyme, ranging across a number of genres, including doggerel, satire, religious tes-timony, sexual boasting, social protest, and seduction. Few songs maintain a consistent tone; many artists boast that they do not. "A thousand styles in one verse," brags Rakim.[27] An extremely minor form in contemporary poetry, doggerel abounds in hip hop. Doggerel serves it so well because prosodic satire and parody rely on an established sense of metrical and rhyming decorum, which the contemporary print-based poetry notably lacks. To register a "*protest* against the inadequacy, against the positive faultiness, of the regular prosody of the time" (*HEP*, 394), the poet needs a "regular prosody" to protest.

Lupe Fiasco's "Hip Hop Saved My Life," for instance, depends on the listener's identifying the hip-hop conventions it evokes. As the title suggests, the song describes a familiar hip-hop figure, introduced as "my homie with the dream": an aspiring artist who wants to raise his family out of poverty. The song's opening describes his goal:

> He said I write what I see
> Write to make it right, don't like where I be.
> I like to make it like the sights on TV
> Quite the great life, so nice and easy.[28]

Asked to describe his style, Fiasco mentions a "simple complexity." "I always want it to seem simple on the surface," he notes, "but if you listen or try to listen—which most cats don't do—but if you really listen, you'll see."[29] In "Hip Hop Saved My Life," deceptively simple rhymes and a pinched vocabulary describe a complex situation. The song plays with its monosyllabic language, squeezing thirty-three words into thirty-seven syllables. "He said I write what I see," the unnamed figure advises, as if hip hop requires only the unmediated witness. However, the pun "write"/"right" suggests that writing might offer a form of transformation and redress, not merely reportage. The second pun, "I *like* to make it *like*/The sights on tv," (my italics) recovers the longing buried within the trope. Any poetry student can define a simile as the comparison of two unlike things, but in practice readers tend to overlook the unlikeness for the shared property. In other words, we focus on how the two things are similar, neglecting their essential difference. With its understated punning wordplay, Fiasco's simile recalls what similes generally smooth over: how the tenor differs from the vehicle and, in the song's case, how the speaker's reality remains unlike the "sights" that inspire him.

To succeed, satiric doggerel must perform a contradictory task, mocking techniques both current and outmoded. Later in the stanza, Fiasco describes the song that the aspiring artist records:

> A bass heavy medley with a sample from the 70s
> With a screwed up hook that went
> STACK THAT CHEESE
> Somethin' somethin' somethin'

Faced with this apparently unpromising material, Fiasco repeats it, adding some filler:

> Mother sister cousin
> STACK THAT CHEESE
> He couldn't think of nothin'
> STACK THAT CHEESE. ("HH")

Like many hip-hop songs, the song within "Hip Hop Saved My Life" presents a hook, a catchy refrain of street slang: in this case, "stack that cheese," meaning to make money.

Introducing his hook for the final time in "Jesus Walks," Kanye West boasts, "Next time I'm in the club everybody screaming out" "Jesus walks."[30] In West's song, the crowd's recognition validates his ambition; he crafts a line that fans shout back wherever he goes. In "Hip Hop Saved My Life," Fiasco shows this aspiration's smallness. He criticizes coolness as a goal, detailing the song's success in less glamorous venues: "Eleven hundred friends on his Myspace page/Stack That Cheese got seven hundred plays" ("HH"). Such listeners mistake bad music for good, admiring what they should ignore. To protest against this prevalent bad taste, "Hip Hop Saved My Life" uses a doggerel structure, a song stripped to its most basic, crowd-pleasing element, "a screwed hook": "Somethin' somethin' somethin'/STACK THAT CHEESE." In an evocative rhyme, "somethin'" turns into "nothin'," a lack of artistic invention, because the entire song within the song exists for its hook.

As another song on the same album more bluntly asserts, Fiasco associates the technique of the hook with commercial pandering. In the chorus of "Dumb It Down," the hip-hop artist repeatedly receives the following advice:

> You putting me to sleep, nigga. (Dumb it down.)
> That's why you ain't popping in the streets nigga.
>   (Dumb it down.)
> You ain't winning no awards, nigga. (Dumb it down).[31]

Resisting these pressures, Fiasco declares, "I flatly refuse" ("DD"). "Hip Hop Saved My Life" works more slyly. Instead of directly stating its artistic principles, the song achieves a simple complexity. The two hooks resemble each other grammatically; each consists of a three-syllable, three-word command. One hook answers the other. "Stack that cheese" satisfies those who demand he "dumb it down" but does so with a wink and a nod to those who "really listen."

In his doggerel, Fiasco fights bad taste. More commonly, though, doggerel exploits bad taste's powerful appeals. Much doggerel entertains the suspicion that its critics might be right, though for the wrong reasons: the lurid pleasures that the rhymes offer might prove unhealthy, if not destructive. In "Ignorant Shit," Jay-Z rhymes his critics' censure with impressively vulgar street insults from two languages, English and Spanish:

> This is that ignorant shit you like:
> nigga fuck shit ass bitch trick precise.
> I got that ignorant shit you love:
> nigga fuck shit maricón puta and drugs.

Addressing his critics, Jay-Z taunts them for their admonishments:

> I got that ignorant shit you need:
> nigga fuck shit ass bitch trick plus weed.
> I'm only trying to give you what you want:
> nigga fuck shit ass bitch you like it don't front![32]

The even lines apparently confirm the most common charges leveled against hip hop: that it presents nothing more than mindless obscenity, namely, base expressions of misogyny, homophobia, and violent aggression—or, in Jay-Z's terms, "ignorant shit." Entire lines list the roughest vulgarity. As if English lacked the resources necessary to curse with sufficient force, Jay-Z turns to street Spanish, insulting both male and female sexuality. While Fiasco presents hip hop as an alternative to drug dealing, Jay-Z presents a more traditional figure: the artist as drug dealer. While some songs praise music for its healing force, "when it hits, you feel no pain,"[33] Jay-Z describes it as an illicit drug that turns listeners into addicts: "crack music," as Kanye West similarly calls it.[34]

In "Ignorant Shit," rhyme recasts criticism into celebration. It focuses furious vulgarity, the nightmare of conventional decorum, into a shapely form. In the song's metaphor, the words resemble a well-cut drug: "precise." To achieve this effect, the rhymes pair desire and fulfillment—"like," "love," "need," and "want"—with what the listener seeks: "precise," "drugs," "weed," and "front." In the anomalous final rhyme, "want"/"front," Jay-Z taunts his critics for their hypocrisy: "you like it, don't front." In a more representative gesture, Jay-Z faces the challenge of finding a rhyme for "love," a notoriously difficult task. Bending pronunciation, he rhymes "love" with "drugs." As in this example, the rhymes seek to thrill. Comic and serious, they render intentional doggerel indistinguishable from real.

In Nas's phrase, both Jay-Z and Lupe Fiasco "carry on tradition";[35] they claim an artistic lineage, complete with characteristic techniques, canonical figures, and distinctive motifs, a situation in which doggerel thrives. Each performer borrows and transforms. Within the last few decades, hip hop has achieved a great sophistication, growing into the early twentieth century's defining culture: "an international phenomenon of imitation, reaction, and general influence that in its most common form is obvious to the point of parody."[36] As in this characterization of Renaissance Petrarchism, hip hop provides a distinctive period style, including identifiable modes of expression. The ubiquity of hip-hop parodies reinforces the music's influence, able to accommodate Ali G's mock interviews and The Roots' video for "What They Do," a deft parody of hip-hop video conventions. Mockingly reproducing techniques from what it calls "Rap Video Manual," the band members sip ginger ale disguised as champagne and watch bikini-clad dancers grind beside the pool of a rented mansion. Knowledge of the genre's traditions establishes an artist's credentials; ignorance discredits performer and listener alike. "I got an exam, let's see if y'all pass it," raps Nas. "Let's see who can quote a Daddy Kane line the fastest" ("COT"). In this musical "exam," allusion combines challenge and homage. If the listener cannot swiftly quote a Daddy Kane line, he fails, not Daddy Kane, whose excellence remains undisputed. "I kick it with the OG's/And listen to the oldies," a young rapper boasts on his debut album, recognizing that hip-hip mastery requires historical knowledge.[37] To "carry on tradition," an artist must learn it. His apprenticeship, though, involves a certain irony: the "oldies" he studies date back only a few decades, recorded in what is commonly called hip hop's "golden age," most commonly defined as the mid-1980s and early 1990s.[38] A young art, hip hop has achieved a startlingly quick maturity, aided by new recording and distribution technologies. Backed by these advances, hip hop's techniques have grown pyrotechnic and allusive. Following the genre's dazzling development, the current moment offers the richest resources and inspires the greatest accomplishment. We are living in hip hop's golden age.

Two examples clarify the advantages that hip hop currently enjoys. In *Cosmopolis*, Don DeLillo eulogizes Brutha Fez, a fictional rapper "born Raymond Gathers in the Bronx."[39] Six times in six pages, DeLillo quotes Fez's songs, "his own vocal adaptations of ancient Sufi music, rapping in Punjabi and Urdu and in the black-swagger English of the street." The first example consists of a quatrain with three-stress lines and a terminal rhyme:

Gettin' shot is easy
Tried it seven times
Now I'm just a solo poet
Workin' on my rhymes (*C*, 133)

The lyrics deeply impress Eric Packer, a billionaire asset manager, as he watches Fez's funeral procession from inside his limousine. Humbled by the experience, Packer notes, "Here was a spectacle he could clearly not command"(*C*, 136). Fez's music dispirits Packer until he weeps uncontrollably. His sorrow arises from an obscure source. Packer weighs his area of expertise, international capital, against Fez's rhymes, judging them to be more vital, expressive, and complex.

The funeral scene evokes two kinds of envy: a character's and a novelist's. While Packer jealously views the "spectacle" Fez can "command," DeLillo, depicting a financier married to a poet, wonders whether hip hop might be the superior art, more capable of addressing the culture's possibilities than the novel, poetry, or financial "data." Yet DeLillo also thinks of hip hop as a kind of artless art, one easily faked. Hip-hop artists typically stress the training they undergo to develop their rhyming skills and the effort each song takes. "I'd be lying if I said it was easy," Eminem admits. "Sometimes I'll spend hours on a single rhyme, or days, or I'll give up and come back to it later. Anyone who says they write a verse in less than 20 minutes is full of shit."[40] Brutha Fez raps about a similar determination to develop his talent. Setting aside his character's insight, DeLillo writes the rhymes that

Fez performs, instead of simply describing them or quoting a song. This strategy is not unique. In Tom Wolfe's *I Am Charlotte Simmons*, college basketball players listen to the music of "Doctor Dis." The novel includes a dozen lines from what it calls "the most rebellious, offensive, vile, obnoxious rap available on CDs," lyrics so extreme that one character wonders if "Doctor Dis himself was a cynic who created this stuff as a parody of the genre."[41] Raising this possibility, Wolfe struts for his readers, pleased to show that he, an elderly, white dandy, can write lyrics as awful as those the teenagers admire. Wolfe's cynical parody differs from DeLillo's anxious homage; it conveys condescension, not ambivalence. A keen observer of contemporary culture, DeLillo wishes to show his mastery of hip-hop technique, to reassert his art against it and reclaim the novel's status. The lyrics, though, lack any animating quality, let alone the trilingual energy that their introduction promises. Their "black-swagger English" sounds more studied than street, more whiny than assertive, casting Fez as a lesser 50 Cent down to the number of wounds he suffered: seven, not nine. They closely resemble Justice Blackmun's verse, using the plural form of the same rhymes, but without the judge's wit. Presenting hip hop as easy, DeLillo, a prose stylist, writes charmless, unintentional doggerel.

Of course, some highly skilled poets employ patterned rhyme, but they typically do so shyly. They favor enjambment, a technique to diminish the rhyme's prominence. A means of concealment, enjambment addresses a potential embarrassment, allowing the rhymes to pass without too much fuss: seen, perhaps, but only faintly heard. Doggerel, though, requires a flamboyance that strains contemporary poetry's resources. When researching *Practical*

Criticism, I. A. Richards famously provided his students with poems that lacked a title, author, or date. To consider the predicament that a poet who writes doggerel faces, briefly I will borrow Richards's method. Consider the following poem, which denounces a proposal to expand faith-based education, without the help of the poem's author or title:

Oh for the pure Intellectual Fever
Of Halal Madresseh and Kosher Yeshiva

Where every last pupil's exactly like you
And with only one Answer it *has* to be true

Oh for the play of Disinterested Mind
The impartial inquiry you're certain to find

Where a Catholic Priest can tell you what's what
And ensure that you can never encounter a Prot

Where a Protestant Elder can call you to order
And assure you the Pope should be swimming in ordure

Oh for the stirring sanguinary stories
That admonish us all with Our Martyrs' past glories

Oh for the splendors of Faith-Based Education
That spread Fear and Hatred throughout the whole Nation.[42]

It is safe to say that Richards's students would heartily condemn this poem. The students, Richards noticed, disliked off-rhyme, denouncing any examples as "poor rhymes."[43] Richards offered two main reasons for this tendency. Because the students never learned how to rhyme competently, they admired poets who accomplish what they could not and treated with "great severity" (*PC*, 34) those whose verse at least superficially resembled their own efforts. "Success or failure for the neophyte is very largely a question of the control of rhymes," Richards realized: "An exaggerated respect for rhyming ability is the result" (34). Second, the students criticized off-rhyme because of their "desire for something tangible by which to judge poetic merit" (34):

> Normal sensibilities can decide with considerable certainty whether two sounds rhyme perfectly or not. The task is nearly as simple as that of a carpenter measuring planks. It is a grateful relief to pass from the nebulous world of intellectual and emotional accordances to definite questions of sensory fact. By assuming that the poet intended to rhyme perfectly, we get a clear unambiguous test for his success or failure. (34)

Contemporary literary criticism does not offer "a clear unambiguous test" for "success or failure." The poem's author, Dick Davis, a distinguished translator and writer of metrical verse, safeguards his lines with an excessive scrupulousness, emphasizing the techniques that Richards removed and I briefly set aside. The extensive title, "William MacGonagall Welcomes the Initiative for a Greater Role for Faith-Based Education," sets the genre. As it indicates, Davis openly borrows from "the King of Doggerel," who, as Davis reports, "has the dubious reputation of being 'the writer of the worst poetry in English'" (*TS*, 53). In the title and the endnote, Davis twice identifies the poem's inspiration as if to protect himself against the accusation that he writes "real" doggerel. Yet the poem lacks the "outrageous, shocking" force that intentional doggerel conveys. Davis borrows the style of a poet dead for more than a century. Addressing current political realities, he longs for a literary culture that would recognize his "rhymes" as "bad." A sense of loss infuses the verse. For the purposes of intentional doggerel such as Davis's, a simple method of appreciating rhyme is better than no method at all.

A peculiar incident clarifies why Davis took such care. In 2007 Billy Collins published "Paradelle for Susan," in the *American Scholar*, the magazine of the Phi Beta Kappa Society. The poem opens:

> I remember the quick, nervous bird of your love.
> I remember the quick, nervous bird of your love.
> Always perched on the thinnest, highest branch.
> Always perched on the thinnest, highest branch.
> Thinnest love, remember the quick branch.
> Always nervous, I perched on your highest bird the.[44]

An author's note explains the form:

> The paradelle is one of the more demanding French fixed forms, first appearing in the *langue d'oc* love poetry of the eleventh century. It is a poem of four six-line stanzas in which the first and second lines, as well as the third and fourth lines of the first three stanzas, must be identical. The fifth and sixth lines, which traditionally resolve these stanzas, must use *all* the words from the preceding lines and *only* those words. Similarly, the final stanza must use every word from *all* the preceding stanzas and *only* those words. (*TP*, 9)

Inspired by the paradelle, Theresa M. Welford, a professor of creative writing, composed a number of her own poems in the form. She also asked Collins if he would like to coedit an anthology of new poems in the form. When he agreed, she invited over 150 poets to participate in the project, and many started to compose their own paradelles.

Of course, the poem was a hoax, as Collins eventually confessed. "I was confident," he explains, "that enough readers would see the poem for what it was: an ironic display of poetic ineptitude, and more broadly, a parody of formal poetry itself, at least the inflexibly strict kind.... Boy, was I wrong" (*TP*, 10). Several markers underscore the author's intention: most prominently, the grotesque inversion that ends the opening stanza's final line, "Always nervous, I perched on your highest bird the." More interesting than the poets who failed to discern this "poetic ineptitude" were the readers who recognized it but could not grasp its implications. Before the hoax was revealed, several subscribers wrote to the journal to complain. One noted that the poem did not follow the form's requirements. Cataloging its "apparent violations of the formula," he concluded, "Unless I badly missed the point, I don't find 'Paradelle for Susan' to be a very impressive example of the tour-de-force that a paradelle purports to be."[45] "How could you allow such a shoddy poem to appear in the journal of the Phi Beta Kappa Society of all places?" another charged, clearly aggrieved (*TP*, 10). In Frye's terms, both mistook "intentional" doggerel for "real." They heard the mistakes but could not detect the parody, at least partly because no standard exists to judge contemporary metrical verse. Such conditions discourage doggerel, except perhaps for the most surreptitious kind: where the poet takes revenge on his readers, revealing their ignorance, but only to himself.

With a strong sense of their art form's traditions, hip-hop artists of various skill levels proceed with greater confidence. Committed to rhyme, they emphasize the technique so deeply that doggerel almost inevitably results. Just as hip hop prizes both collaboration and competition, rhyme establishes connections even as an artist asserts his uniqueness. A rhyme echoes and expands; it recalls neighboring sounds and previous uses, and calls for responses. Demonstrating this dynamic, Kanye West's "Gold Digger" starts with a gesture familiar to hip hop: a nostalgic allusion. Jamie Foxx imitates Ray Charles while revising lines from "I Got a Woman." "She take my money when I'm in need/Yeah, she's a trifling friend indeed," Foxx sings, borrowing Charles's rhyme but reversing the meaning.[46] Charles sang, "She give me money when I'm in need/Yeah, she's a kind of friend indeed."[47] This allusion marks an affinity based in a contrast; Foxx longs for the subservient loyalty that Charles celebrates. "Never runnin' in the streets and leavin' me alone," Charles praises his lover, "She knows a woman's place is right there now in her home." Yet the song's light tone presents sexual politics as a farce, not a battle, as the unchanged rhyme marks the song's true desire. To borrow Charles's rhyme is to try on his style.

Midway through "Gold Digger," West introduces a cautionary example, a star pro football player exploited by a "gold digger": "You will see him on TV any given Sunday,/ Win the Super Bowl and drive off in a Hyundai." Instead of enjoying his earnings, the pro football player watches the "gold digger" spend it:

> She was supposed to buy ya shorty Tyco with ya money.
> She went to the doctor got lipo with ya money.
> She walkin' around lookin' like Michael with ya money.
> Shoulda got that insured, GEICO for ya money.

In this highly effective doggerel, each rhyme strains to outdo its predecessor. The opening antonym-rhyme, "Sunday"

and "Hyundai," ironically counterpoints symbols of professional success and financial failure. The football star drives "a
Hyundai," not one of the luxury cars ubiquitous in hip-hop
songs and videos, though he plays on "Sunday," when the
National Football League holds its games. The next rhyme
group contains four instances—two more than the first—
though the rhymes remain trochaic, blurring this division.
The second group's opening rhyme connects childhood and
adult realms: toys and elective surgery, "Tyco" and "lipo." The
next rhyme illustrates this comparison, invoking "Michael"
Jackson, a figure bizarrely caught between childhood and
adulthood, as well as gender and race. Like the passage's
other primarily visual rhyme, "Hyundai," "Michael" evokes
both the image and its contrast: in the case of Jackson, the
difference between his peculiarly refashioned body and earlier versions. The rhymes sketch a comic equation: "Tyco" +
"lipo" = "Michael." Instead of employing rhyme to maintain
distance from contemporary culture, West, like many hip-
hop artists, characteristically uses it to evoke the era's distinctive features, including its celebrities, products, surgical
procedures, and companies. The rhymes couple new inflections and objects of desire, as well as updated grotesqueries
and threats. They mark a sophisticated worldliness, an insid-
er's knowledge of contemporary mores.

The style's availability allows artists to create with breath-
taking speed, exploiting the latest technologies. On September
2, 2005, Kanye West appeared on a fundraiser for the victims
of Hurricane Katrina, broadcast live. Ignoring the prepared
script, he criticized the Bush administration's response to the
disaster and the media's portrayal of it. Appearing beside West,
Mike Myers looked increasingly helpless: a comedian fated to
be the butt of many jokes. Just after West exclaimed, "George

Bush doesn't care about black people!" the cameras cut away.[48] Four days after the benefit, a previously uncelebrated Houston hip-hop duo, the Legendary K.O., posted on their Web site, "George Bush Doesn't Care about Black People," their reworking of "Gold Digger" recorded on home computers and composed through emails and instant messaging. "Within the first 24 hours, it was downloaded 10,000 times," Legendary K.O. member Damien Randle remembered. "It crashed our server."[49] Within days, a freelance video producer in New Brunswick, New Jersey, composed an arresting video and circulated it on the Internet, attracting more attention.

"George Bush Doesn't Care about Black People" recasts the chorus of "Gold Digger," decrying Bush, not a potential lover: "I ain't saying he a gold digger,/but he ain't messing with no broke niggas." Borrowing the "Gold Digger" instrumental, the chorus repeats a more cutting version of West's criticism, asserting again and again, "George Bush don't like black people." "The suggestion that I was a racist because of the response to Katrina represented an all-time low," George W. Bush later recalled. "I told Laura at the time that it was the worst moment of my presidency."[50] The song expands West's charge. In "Gold Digger," West's rhymes display his linguistic and comic inventiveness; they delight in the connections that sound-coincidences allow. Setting the words to West's tune, the Legendary K.O. crafts the same device into a gesture of outrage. The first quatrain announces this strategy in suitably forceful language:

> Hurricane came through, fucked us up round here.
> Government acting like it's bad luck down here.
> All I know is that you better bring some trucks round here.
> Wonder why I got my middle finger up round here.[51]

The stanza moves from skepticism to defiance. The first end-rhyme pair suggests that more than "bad luck" "fucked us up," that is, caused the speaker's misery. Building on this point, the third line cites logistical needs quite separate from misfortune: "trucks" filled with supplies, ready to transport New Orleans residents from the city. In the fourth line, the rhyme changes both in function and in construction, playing with the listener's expectations. Given the rising anger that the lines express, the listener anticipates that the curse "fuck" will return. Instead, the fourth line repeats the preposition "up" that the first line downplays, raising it to a position of prominence. The rhyme pattern also changes, introducing an approximate vowel-rhyme different from the previous full rhymes. Both maneuvers recall the anticipated word's absence. It may seem odd to call a doggerel description of an obscene gesture tactful, but the final line draws significant force from the decision not to repeat the swear. Instead, the rhyme itself strikes the formal equivalent of the depicted gesture: "Wonder why I got my middle finger up round here." A balance of desperation and dignity, the rhyme surprises with its defiant refusal.

As this example suggests, doggerel listens hard to rhyme, trusting it to direct the song's energies. Rhyme openly generates the possibilities that the song pursues. To many, the result may seem uncontrolled or, rather, controlled by the wrong forces. Yet hip hop suggests that doggerel can achieve a surprising flexibility, ranging from the comic to the serious, from the delicate to the vulgar. It would be a mistake, though, to say the technique determines the result. Rather, hip hop hungers for rhymes; it feeds on nearly whatever it can find. Such doggerel lays bare the machinery of its making, amplifying the process that poetry typically conceals: how an environment of rhyme turns into art.

THE ART OF RHYMED INSULT

IN 1991, ELVIS MITCHELL, NATIONAL Public Radio's weekend entertainment reporter, interviewed Spike Lee for *Playboy* magazine. "Lee," Mitchell informed his readers, "has made my life miserable for the past couple of months":

> [I]nvariably, in phone-tag intramurals preceding our meetings, every message Lee left on my answering machine began with those deathless words, followed by his trademark cackle.[1]

The "deathless words" that unnerved Mitchell were not Lee's own. Gleefully the filmmaker quoted a canonical hip-hop insult, the opening lines of Public Enemy's "Fight the Power," rapped by Chuck D and made internationally famous by Lee's film, *Do the Right Thing:*

> Elvis was a hero to most,
> but he never meant shit to me, you see.
> Straight out racist, that sucker was, simple and plain.[2]

Clinching the rhyme, Flavor Flav adds, "Mother fuck him and John Wayne." "Fight the Power" features a sledgehammer rhyme, blunt and heavy, but does so with surprising delicacy. The monosyllabic rhymes, "me"/"see," and "plain"/"Wayne," are linguistically uncomplicated, as if simply revealing a hard

truth, a "simple and plain" fact, not a debatable allegation.[3]
The lines, though, powerfully develop a rather intricate pattern, as the epithets build in vehemence, until sealed with
the final insult, one of the very coarsest that English offers.
Chuck D's lines move from the opening honorific "hero,"
mentioned twice, to a series of denigrations that assault Elvis
as "shit," "racist," and "sucker." Each lowers Elvis's status until
Flavor Flav's line obliterates it. The final rhyme adds vehemence to these harsh dismissals. It embodies the anger that
the words express.

"Poetry of bad personal feeling, insult, revenge," observes
Robert Pinsky. "It's central to the art."[4] It is marginal, though,
to the art of contemporary poetry. Insult flourishes in rhyming cultures, whether in nonliterary venues such as Turkish
boys' rhyming duels and American playgrounds or in particular literary eras.[5] In Augustan satire, a literary historian
notes, "abuse is made art; a hyperbole of insult is wedded
to a malicious realism," while another scholar describes
the Restoration's "idiom of insult and injury," "the verbal,
even physical, violence that often defined the life of letters
in late seventeenth-century London."[6] Such strategies revise
a longer-standing practice. In the early modern "culture of
slander," for instance, rhymed verse so frequently served as a
vehicle for slander that "defamation" was "increasingly associated with poetry."[7] In such eras, insult verse represents a
major genre in English-language poetry as well as a challenge
to many high-minded justifications of the art. Few contemporary print-based poets, though, write insult verse.[8] In a historical moment when a certain mode dominates print-based
poetry, namely, lyric characterized by meditative sensitivity, it is easy to forget how many of the language's canonical authors—including Chaucer, Shakespeare, Ben Jonson,

Pope, Dryden, and Yeats—wrote scabrous, mean-spirited verse. They delighted in insult verse's vituperative pleasures. If "[p]oetry of bad personal feeling, insult, revenge" is "central to the art," hip-hop artists, not contemporary poets, claim the center.

Committed to rhyme, hip-hop artists explore how the technique's structures and properties serve insult verse's combative ambitions. "Rhyme," Roman Jakobson remarked in a classic formulation, "is only a particular, condensed case of a much more general, we may even say the fundamental, problem of poetry, namely *parallelism*."[9] Insult verse employs parallelism in order to sharpen an opposition. One element discredits the other, as the rhyme insists on the essential difference of two similar elements. "Fight the Power," for instance, contrasts "most" and "me," to set off those who celebrate Elvis as a "hero" from the figure of Chuck D who condemns him. Finishing the rhyme, Flavor Flav seals the distinction as the rhyme marks a shared value against a morally skewed world. "People, people we are the same," Chuck D raps, only to turn against this tolerant view, "No, we're not the same/Cause we don't know the game" ("FP"). In much insult verse, the technique forms a barrier as well as an invitation. Rhyme intensifies and illuminates antagonisms; it separates like-minded individuals from their opponents, claiming allies and abusing adversaries.

To do so, hip-hop insult verse exploits rhyme's basic unfairness. In one of its great strengths, insult rhyme need not explain; it insinuates, calling to mind unsavory associations without fully acknowledging them. When Spike Lee rapped "Fight the Power" into Mitchell's answering machine, the critic's first name, "Elvis," made him an easy target. In one sense, Lee opportunistically turns Mitchell's name into a nonsensical taunt, based on nothing more than the coincidence that Mitchell shares it with Presley. Public Enemy targets the singer, not the reporter. The borrowed words, though, cut deeper. When Lee raps, "Elvis was a hero to most/But he never meant shit to me, you see," he distinguishes between himself and Mitchell's parents, for whom Elvis presumably meant a great deal: enough, perhaps, to name their child after him or at least to have their child share Presley's name. Like Lee, Mitchell is black, yet he bears the name of a man whom Public Enemy dismisses as "Straight out racist, that sucker was, simple and plain." Repeating the rhyme, Lee contrasts the Mitchell family's putative self-hatred with the racial pride that Public Enemy promotes. If, as Chuck D later explained, "[t]he attack was directed toward the *institution* of Elvis," Lee places Mitchell within that institution.[10] In the song's terms, the rhyme positions Mitchell as part of the "power" that we must "fight." Just as Lee never explicitly states the quotation's point, he need not finish the insult verse to let the rhyme do its work. Such insinuations, unstated and therefore nearly impossible to rebut, prove maddening. In insult verse, the accuracy of the charge matters less than its confident presentation. To be assertive is to be right; to be memorable is to win. Exploiting such unfair rules, Lee's needling performance, punctuated with a cackle, achieved the desired effect of making Mitchell's "life miserable."

As in this example, rhyme's sound structures make an insult hard to laugh off, no matter how inaccurate. Rhyme, Schopenhauer reported, inspires "blind consent to what is read...and this gives the poem a certain emphatic power of conviction."[11] The technique adds a persuasive rhetorical force that may escape the reader's conscious attention.

Rhyme makes words sound persuasive, regardless of their meaning. Consider Run-D.M.C.'s famous boast:

> I stepped on stage, at Live Aid.
> All the people gave and the poor got paid.[12]

The couplet features a synonym-rhyme, with the rhyme words, "Live Aid" and "paid," rendered as equivalent.[13] The Ethiopian relief–fundraising concert "Live Aid" means the "poor got paid." The assertion sounds correct, unarguably and assuredly so, as the confident rhyme clinches the argument. In Schopenhauer's terms, the rhyme exacts the listener's "blind consent." Based in a sonic coincidence, Run-D.M.C.'s rhyme performs a neat trick: it makes an ultimately failed goal sound already achieved. Investigating how international agencies distributed Live Aid–funded relief in Ethiopia, David Rieff laments, "[T]here is no necessary connection between raising a lot of money for a good cause and spending that money well."[14] As Rieff notes, controversies remain over how many lives the aid saved and how many deaths it hastened, because of the government's use of these funds for its own purposes. Given such questions, the couplet more accurately might read:

> I stepped on stage, at Live Aid.
> All the people gave, but the poor weren't paid.

The revised couplet suggests rhyme's essential arbitrariness: the rhyme pair might advance one argument or the opposite. Run-D.M.C recorded "My Adidas" within a year of Live Aid, expressing the moment's optimism; the rhyme presents a hope as a realized fact. It affirms a missing connection, making an arguable point seem self-evident. The artful rhyme shows how easily a fictive technique passes as the bearer of truth.

Rhyme works well for insult verse because it seeks to provoke a reaction, not to prove a point. Rhymes protest and enliven previous ones by creating new uses: new distinctions, agreements, and contestations. A successful rhyme demands another. "Fight the Power" draws from Clarence Reid, who performed outrageously cartoonish, sexually explicit songs under the name of Blowfly. ("You is nastier than a blowfly," he reports his grandmother calling him.)[15] In his best-known song, "Rap Dirty," Blowfly describes a black trucker dueling with the grand dragon of the Ku Klux Klan:

> He said, "Listen nigger man,
> I'm the grand dragon of the Ku Klux Klan."
> He said, "There`s no nigger badder than me.
> Mother fuck you and Muhammad Ali."[16]

"I reversed the charges," Chuck D remembers, meaning that when he wrote "Fight the Power," he borrowed the syntax and structure of Blowfly's line but redirected the insult so that the black speaker attacks a white racist, instead of a white racist attacking the black speaker.[17] The lines, though, perform more than a simple reversal. The borrowed syntactical structure carries significant power; a line starting with an active trochaic verb bursts with grammatical and metrical energy. In "Fight the Power," the aggressive syntactical structure amplifies the anger that the obscenity conveys. The rhyme also records the lines' genealogy. Public Enemy's introduction, "but he never meant shit to me, you see," rhymes with Blowfly's opening, "He said, 'There's no nigger badder than me.'" The sound marks a train of association, an affinity. As hip hop developed in the 1980s, Blowfly formed a model for a generation of artists who followed his injunction to "rap dirty"; they parodied popular songs with raunchy versions, crafting apprentice exercises designed to gain attention in the underground music scene. Blowfly inspired Public Enemy differently. More earnest than bawdy, the rappers use Blowfly's scatological techniques in order to register outrage. They employ the language deliberately, reserving the curse Blowfly freely employs for a crucial moment. Whereas "Rap Dirty" refers a half-dozen times to "motherfucker," "Fight the Power" does so only once in order to level its most provocative charge, "Mother fuck him and John Wayne." In "Rap Dirty," the scatological language is the norm. In Blowfly's outlandish parodies, the language satirizes the very notion of good taste. In "Fight the Power" the same word conveys a moral force.

"Fight the Power" uses rhyme against rhyme; it fights another use of the same technique. In the following lines, Public Enemy defines its artistic ambition:

"Don't Worry Be Happy" was a number one jam.
Damn, if I say it, you can slap me right here.
(Get it) Let's get this party started right. ("FP")

While it refers to Bobby McFerrin's song with journalistic specificity, "Fight the Power" makes no mention of its immediate inspiration: the title song of Paul Simon's album, *Graceland*, winner of the 1988 Grammy for Record of the Year, which depicts a pilgrimage to Presley's home. The omission signals a certain disdain. Simon remains simply one of the "most" to whom Elvis served as "a hero." By not naming Simon, Public Enemy treats him as unexceptional and uninteresting, no more than one example of a broader pattern. Few listeners, though, failed to recognize the song as an attack on Simon's "Graceland," which depicts Elvis as an American cultural hero. Public Enemy treats McFerrin as a proxy for Simon, an easier target than Simon's more allusive, sophisticated rhyming. The substitution deepens the insult, presenting "Don't Worry Be Happy" as indistinguishable from "Graceland."

A focus for the group's anger, "Don't Worry Be Happy" represents the kind of complacent "party music" that Public Enemy disdains. In McFerrin's song, rhyme reinforces the carefree attitude that the lines promote; the technique adds a tone of willed blitheness. "Here's a little song I wrote," the song self-deprecatingly opens:

> You might want to sing it note for note.
> In every life we have some trouble.
> Don't worry, be happy.
> But when you worry you make it double.[18]

The speaker repeats the rhymes as if to hold off his unspecified difficulties; to mention them would be to accept their reality. McFerrin's rhymes soothe and alleviate the "trouble" he and his listeners endure. Public Enemy ridicules this stance, turning McFerrin's words against him. In a strategy familiar to insult verse, one rhyme discredits another by making it sound wrong. When Public Enemy rhymes "happy" and "slap me," they transform McFerrin's key word into a joke. The antonym rhyme rejects McFerrin's advice; instead of calm serenity, Public Enemy values excitement: "I'm ready and hyped plus I'm amped" ("FP"), another line heatedly announces, piling adjectives upon each other. Like the action it describes, a man begging his friend to slap him if he ever utters the seemingly innocuous words "don't worry, be happy," the mosaic rhyme exaggerates its stance into comedy. Cobbling together three words into a rhyme pair, the couplet sounds both menacing and playful. Even more than the line that follows, it announces Public Enemy's aim to create an alternative form of party music, neither escapist nor simply vulgar, neither "Don't Worry Be Happy" nor "Rap Dirty." The rhyme, though, does not carry the incendiary power of the earlier lines. Buried within the verse, it remains only faintly heard.

Instead, the song's louder, sharper rhymes provoked the greatest reaction, challenges that reinforced their canonical status. Two examples suggest how insult rhymes demand responses, how an attack proves the original rhyme's power. In "Elvis Is Dead," Living Colour quoted "Fight the Power" in order to qualify its claim:

> Elvis was a hero to most
> But that's beside the point.
> A black man taught him how to sing
> and then he was crowned king.[19]

Such rhymes reinforce Public Enemy's lines instead of displacing them. Living Colour quotes the opening of the passage in "Fight the Power," but whereas Public Enemy personalizes the issue—"he never meant shit to me"—Living Colour strikes a cooler, more impersonal tone. Their anticlimactic second line eschews rhyme in order to offer a qualifying aside: "But that's beside the point." In the following couplet, fourteen monosyllabic words offer an accusation. Instead of the aggressive syntax and language that Public Enemy borrows from Blowfly, Living Colour uses a blander compound construction. They seek to correct the record, a stance that insult verse poorly serves. Public Enemy's lines sting; Living Colour's verse quibbles.

Pursing a craftier strategy, U2 borrows a rhyme to revise the words' meanings. In "Elvis Ate America," U2 recasts Chuck D's insult into doggerel:

> Elvis… the public enemy
> Elvis… don't mean shit to Chuck D.
> Elvis… changed the center of gravity.[20]

In a seemingly casual phrase, U2 calls Elvis "the public enemy." As the definite article suggests, Elvis defined this outlaw identity. The ordering is crucial; as in the rhyme, Elvis precedes Chuck D. The rhyme identifies Elvis as the originator and his harshest critic as an imitator. "Chuck D" rhymes with "the public enemy"; the rapper wants to place himself in opposition to Presley, but the rhyme insists that he comes second. Chuck D may protest that Elvis "don't mean shit," but the rhyme records Chuck D's indebtedness, making the group's swaggering name sound almost laughable. When the rapper calls himself a "public enemy," he unwittingly pays homage to the singer he attacks.

U2's rhyme treads lightly along a racial divide. The debate extends beyond the question of whether Elvis unfairly appropriated certain elements of black culture; it includes the very notion of rhyme itself. Rhyme has long been associated with African-American culture and its most prominent forms of artistic expression. In his landmark study, *Negro Folk Rhymes: Wise and Otherwise*, Thomas W. Talley, often credited as the first African-American folklorist, noted "[t]hat the Negro of savage Africa has the rhyme-making habit and probably has always had it, and thus the American Negro brought this habit with him to America."[21] Using different terms, more recent scholarship traces a line of artistic and cultural development that runs through African griots, toasts, preaching traditions, the dozens, and musical forms such as soul, funk, blues, and hip hop.[22] "The love of rhyme," the folklorist Daryl Cumber Dance concludes, "is a given in Black communities."[23] While "[t]he love of rhyme" might constitute a cultural "given," the technique does not remain solely within black communities. Rhymes cross races and travel distances, open to new inflections, whether deferential, playful, or hostile. Paradoxically, this mobility intensifies the technique's ability to summon racial allegiances.

Alan Vinegrad, the US attorney for the Eastern District of New York, showed a keen appreciation of this potential when he prosecuted Lemrick Nelson Jr. The case endured a long and complicated history driven by New York's racial, religious, and political tensions.[24] In August 1991 a car driven by an Orthodox Jew following the motorcade of Rabbi Menachem Mendel Schneerson, the head of the Lubavitch Chasidic Court, accidently hit two black children, killing a seven-year-old boy and seriously injuring his young cousin. News quickly spread through the Crown Heights neighborhood, an overwhelmingly black community where Lubavitch Jews comprised a small but highly visible minority. A crowd gathered at the accident scene, angered by the incident and what they saw as the preferential treatment that the neighborhood's Jews received. Four days of rioting followed. A few hours after the accident, Yankel Rosenbaum, a yeshiva student, was stabbed; the next morning he died. The police arrested Lemrick Nelson Jr., a black teenager, after he was found wearing bloody pants and carrying a bloody knife. In 1992 a jury acquitted Nelson on state murder charges. Amid much legal wrangling, in 1997 Nelson was tried in federal court for violating the civil rights of Yankel Rosenbaum.

A particular moment of courtroom theater enlivened the trial. Nelson's attorney arranged for him to try on the pants that the government charged he had worn when he killed Rosenbaum. Quickly they fell to the floor, leading Nelson's attorney to charge that the evidence was planted. In his closing argument Vinegrad attacked this position:

> What [does the defense] resort to? The baggy-pants defense. Until today the fiascoes of the case on the West Coast—I won't mention the name—hadn't invaded this trial. But the defense in his desperation brought it into the courtroom and paraded it before you. It turned the courtroom into the theater of the absurd. Pants don't fit, you must acquit. That is what you would have heard from that table. You know what? They are wrong. They are baggy. Like it's a big surprise that teenagers in Brooklyn in the 1990s would walk around with big baggy pants on. I am sure that is a big shock to everybody here.
>
> All that Lemrick Nelson's demonstration here proves is, he wears baggy pants. Over the last five and a half years, either these well-traveled pants have gotten stretched out a bit or he's gotten more slender or firmer or both. Who knows? Maybe that is why the police were able to catch him, because he couldn't run fast enough, because of holding on to these baggy pants. I guess what I am really saying, since that California case is in the courtroom now, "If the pants don't fit, I don't give a ." You fill in the rest.[25]

Vinegrad engages a rhyming battle not only with the defense but with the racially coded technique of rhyming itself. The US attorney's words recall America's most famous legal rhyme, Johnnie Cochran's much-quoted recommendation to the jury in the O.J. Simpson trial, "If it [the glove] doesn't fit, you must acquit." After Simpson's acquittal, some observers saw the couplet as deviously good, inspiring the jurors to ignore the other evidence. A writer of a grammar textbook, for instance, maintained that the rhyme "worked magic" on the jurors, while a guide to persuasion cited Cochran's rhyme, noting, "Rhyme creates believability."[26] By the time of Nelson's second trial, Cochran's rhyme had become the subject of countless parodies, some by Cochran himself. "I am unhappy to admit," Cochran lamented, his sorrow lightened with more than a touch of pride, "that few people have done as much for truly bad rhyming as I have."[27] According to his self-description, Vinegrad preempts the defense's bad rhyming, "Pants don't fit, you must acquit. That is what you would have heard from that table," labeling it with the cutting phrase, "The baggy-pants defense." As with this clownish stereotype of black urban youth, a criminal caught "because he couldn't run fast enough, because of holding on to these baggy pants," Vinegrad recalls a literary technique's racial associations and recent past.

Revising Cochran's words, Vinegrad reworks their history. His rhyme depends on the jurors' participation in it. To introduce this task, Vinegrad mentions "the fiascoes of the case on the West Coast—I won't mention the name." As if mentioning the Simpson case aloud were too indelicate, Vinegrad does not lower himself to identify it. He presents Simpson's name as a tawdriness akin to the rhyme's expletive (but unvoiced) "shit": to say either would be to debase oneself as well as the court. By doing so, Vinegrad seeks to shift responsibility to the defense, who "brought it [the Simpson case] into the courtroom and paraded it before you." Vinegrad blames the defense for the rhyme he uses.

Despite his conspicuously staged good manners, Vinegrad turned the courtroom into a venue resembling a schoolyard. Analyzing schoolyard taunts, Martha Wolfenstein shrewdly notes how rhyme diminishes the speaker's responsibility:

> What is the function of rhymes in these joking attacks? I would suggest that the first rhyming word has the effect of compelling the utterance of the second, thus reducing the speaker's responsibility....[A] more advanced maneuver consists in inducing the victim to utter the first rhyming word, to which the joker then joins the rhymed insult. Once the first word has been spoken, it is as if the rhyming word has been commanded. There is a further reduction of responsibility in the use of a learned formula: The words are not my own. Moreover the rhyme is apt to induce other children to take it up; the attacker will cease to be alone.[28]

Vinegrad's rhyme works similarly. The rhyming formula reduces his responsibility, especially since, as he charges, the defense bears the responsibility for the rhyme. The words are not the speaker's, the formula asserts: they belong to Cochran and to the defense (who never uttered them) because "[t]hat is what you would have heard from that table." As we have seen, one of rhyme's great strengths remains its capability to work by implication, by setting in place a chain of associations without explicitly committing to any. Rhyme asks listeners to "fill in the rest," whether context, implication, or particular words. The sonic echo draws parallels. Vinegrad's rhyme implies that a guilty verdict in the Nelson case would offer a judgment against Simpson, even though few connections exist between the two cases except the defendants' race. When the jurors finish the rhyme of "fit" and "shit," they complete the prosecutor's assertion that the Simpson defense, like the Nelson defense, was contemptible. In the couplet's logic, to amend Cochran's rhyme is to correct the Simpson verdict.

While an insult rhyme summons allegiances, it also reconfigures them. Hip-hop insult rhyme urges a particular form of persuasion; it transforms the listener's participation into an alliance. One of the most controversial hip-hop songs remains "Fuck tha Police," recorded by NWA (Niggaz with Attitude), condemned by the FBI yet often cited as one of the greatest songs of the 1980s. In a demonstration of the hard postures that rhyme projects, Ice Cube taunts the police for taunting him:

> Fuckin' with me cuz I'm a teenager
> With a little bit of gold and a pager.[29]

The couplet throws back an insult. The two clenched lines connect the speaker's age with the facts that the police use to profile him—"gold and a pager," the jewelry and the technology then at the height of their popularity. Attitude carries the rhyme, a dactyl and a trochee that dare the listener to object. Its force reconfigures the speaker's relation to the police, making them the harassed party and him the aggressor. Ice Cube's couplet enforces a perimeter delineating cops from "Niggaz with Attitudes." Yet the rhyme also extends an invitation. Numerous bands composed of white musicians covered the song and countless white listeners have enjoyed it, a popularity that extends beyond blackface postures. Few of these listeners mistook themselves for black inner-city youth or drug dealers hassled by cops. Articulation, though, changes a listener's relation to the words. To say an insult rhyme is to participate in it, to claim the status of an ally. Rhyme asks for the listener to experience it, not just to hear it. No matter how repellent the subject it explores or how intimidating the stance it strikes, a rhyme aims to be joined.

During the last several decades, as hip hop grew into an international phenomenon, print-based poets have neglected the genre of insult verse. In gatherings and in private conversations, many poets deftly practice related arts: they excel at the gossipy putdown and the caustic assessment of their rivals. The literary culture delights in such lively expressions of ill will. Few contemporary masters of insult poetry exist, however, perhaps for the same reason that few negative reviews of poetry collections appear in print. Professional interests caution against both forms of enemy making.

Contemporary poets prefer to write blurbs, not curse rhymes and maledictions; they do not engage in flytings or other kinds of insult battles. The last master of insult verse, J. V. Cunningham composed fastidious rhymes that preached (as his teacher Yvor Winters summarized) "the doctrine of hatred, or anger," presenting hatred as "the only cleansing emotion and the most moral of emotions."[30] In subject and style, Cunningham deliberately wrote against literary fashion.

On the rare occasions when poets compose insult verse, they typically do so cagily. Consider the following poem written by Anthony Hecht from a series titled "A Little Cemetery":

> Here lies fierce Strephon, whose poetic rage
> Lashed out on Vietnam from page and stage;
> Whereby from basements of Bohemia he

Rose to the lofts of sweet celebrity,
Being, by Fortune, (our Eternal Whore)
One of the few to profit by that war,
A fate he shared—it bears much thinking on—
With certain persons at the Pentagon.[31]

Decades after publishing the poem in the short-lived journal
Counter/Measures, Hecht gratefully told an interviewer who
quoted the poem, "Thank you for exhuming those buried
lines. They do indeed express my impatience of those years
with indignant, sanctimonious poets."[32] Despite his fondness
for the poem, Hecht never collected it; he allowed "the lines"
to be "buried." The verse remains nearly as discreet as its publishing history. Precisely calibrated, the verse depersonalizes
the conflict, condemning a kind of poet more than a particular writer. Unlike previous classics of insult verse such as
"MacFlecknoe" or "The Dunciad," Hecht's verse does not dis-
close whom it attacks. Hecht composed the poem before the
Vietnam War ended, but the poet he addresses, "Strephon,"
lies in the grave, distanced from the contemporary moment.
Apparently the poem's readers appreciate its tact: a scholar of
war poetry approvingly notes the poem condemns a "(fortu-
nately unidentified) armchair poet."[33]

An illuminating exception, Hecht's poem recalls how
rarely contemporary poets compose similar kinds of verse,
let alone harsher versions. In contrast, hip-hop artists show
little reluctance to engage in battle rhymes; they insult each
other with great enthusiasm, inspired by both artistic and
professional motivations. They boast of their art form's
pugnacity. "Can't see no country singers beefing over some
guitar/Riff," Eminem sneers, "that Willie Nelson lifted from
Bob Seger."[34] The most popular form of hip-hop insult verse

remains the particular subgenre that contemporary poets avoid: the attack of artistic rivals. Few hip-hop artists achieve prominence without mastering this art.

Early in his career, for instance, Jay-Z engaged in career-building battles with fellow hip-hop artists such as Tupac Shakur, Nas, and Mobb Deep. More recently, he has attacked antagonists from outside hip hop, suggesting his ambition exceeded its limits. After the news leaked that Jay-Z would headline the Glastonbury music festival, Noel Gallagher, the lead singer for Oasis, complained, "I'm sorry, but Jay-Z? No chance. Glastonbury has a tradition of guitar music.... I don't know about it. But I'm not having hip-hop at Glastonbury. It's wrong."[35] Quickly Jay-Z seized the opportunity that these comments presented, unveiling a new song, "Jockin' Jay-Z":

> That bloke from Oasis said I couldn't play guitar.
> Somebody should have told him I'm a fucking rock star.
> Today is gonna be the day that I'm gonna throw it back
>   to you.[36]

Jay-Z refutes Gallagher's attack by shifting the terms. The rhyme couples "guitar" and "rock star," placing the two in opposition. A conventional metonym of rock-and-roll stardom, the "guitar" suggests its opposite. While Gallagher plays the instrument, Jay-Z rhymes, a performance represented as a greater art and more glamorous lifestyle. Contemptuously Jay-Z calls Gallagher "that bloke from Oasis," as if unable to recall the singer's name, lowering him to the status of an anonymous band member, not a solo artist and celebrity. "I see you jockin' Jay-Z," the opening line asserts, setting envy as the reason for the criticism, "cuz he got a Mercedes/and you know about his ladies" ("JJZ"). More than twenty times the song repeats the hip-hop artist's name, never once mentioning Gallagher's. It proclaims the hip-hop performer's name like a champion's, recalling that its very sound inspires admiration and envy, as "Jay-Z" rhymes with the symbols of rock star status: "Mercedes" and "ladies." The contrast is clear. Nothing glamorous or sexy rhymes with "that bloke from Oasis."

The stanza's last two lines perform another reversal. They quote Gallagher's own words in the opening of Oasis's hit song "Wonderwall": "Today is gonna be the day/that I'm gonna throw it back to you" ("JJZ"). In Oasis's original, the lines present a dreamy putdown, so dreamy in fact that many listeners puzzle over their meaning. Jay-Z's rendition leaves no doubt. Set after the previous insult, the lines promise a payback, which the rest of the song delivers. "Jockin' Jay-Z," though, does not return to Gallagher in order to offer more abuse; it treats him as irrelevant. Instead, it demonstrates what "rock star" means. Jay-Z crafts memorable rhymes that move effortlessly between street life and elegant society. The last stanza shows how Jay-Z resembles the rhymes he crafts, inhabiting two worlds at once:

> I'm so ghetto chic.
> I'm where the hood and high fashion meet.
> Oh, wee. I'm like camouflage Louis.
> How you niggas want it? The tux or the toolie? ("JJZ")

Jay-Z rhymes language from two different spheres: "Louis" Vuitton, the French fashion house, and "toolie," slang for a gun. Like the rhyme, Jay-Z embodies "ghetto chic," equally at home with "the hood and high fashion." A rock star does not need to play an instrument. He demands attention by achieving an outsized life. The song's central pun, "jockin'," possesses two meanings: to attack and to desire sexually. "I got models in the moshpit," "the song boasts, "dancing off beat, but they know the words to my shit" ("JJZ"). A mixture of beauty and awkwardness, "models" approach the stage, trying to catch Jay-Z's attention. The "haters," the artists who wish to displace Jay-Z, work similarly; they know his songs but cannot master their art. "Haters, I ain't mad at you," Jay-Z coolly notes. "If it wasn't me, I'd probably jock me too" ("JJZ"). The "haters" want his life with a longing intense as any erotic desire. Their challenge validates Jay-Z's status because their attention confirms it. Turning this fact against Gallagher, Jay-Z treats him as an anonymous pretender, worth only a quick insult. A veteran battler, Jay-Z makes his wannabe rival disappear.

With such deft maneuvers, Jay-Z recasts the situation into a particular kind of insult rhyme: a battle between star and wannabe. Oasis enjoys an international following; they hardly lack media coverage or public recognition. To diminish Gallagher, Jay-Z calls him one of the "haters," casting him as a little-known musician who attacks a star in order to gain attention. Jay-Z describes a contest between the lowly and the great, not between equals. The desire for fame energizes this kind of rhyme battle; the hopeful seeks the acclaim that the star possesses. In many examples, though, both participants gain from the feud, garnering record sales and attracting media attention. Setting aside such mutual benefits, they describe their interests as wholly opposed. They simplify the contest into a neat equation: one participant gains what the other loses.

In insult-rhyme battles over fame, then, the participants strive to control what their own names and the names of their rivals signify. To lose power over one's name is to suffer a profound vulnerability. No longer does the artist craft his or her identity. Instead, the least sympathetic observer defines it as cruelly and vindictively as possible. In their extensive dispute, Lil' Kim and Foxy Brown vehemently attack each other in songs and interviews, continuing an argument whose origins remain obscure even to music insiders. The battle's existence establishes its main point; it serves as a given in both artists' musical identities. "Hot damn ho, here we go again," Foxy Brown quotes her rival's insult before launching another round of attack:

> Let's be truthful, give a fuck if your album push back,
> or when it hit the streets, bitch, you're still weak.
> You still sound lame, and my name still reign.[37]

Such rhymes signal haughty condescension. According to Foxy Brown, her words achieve an unrivaled power, while Lil' Kim's remain harmless. For this reason, Brown pretends not to care whether Lil' Kim launches another attack. For this strategy to succeed, the verse must "sound" its excellence, establishing the difference between its strength and the opponent's weakness. In the song's own terms, this "truth" must be obvious. Brown's rhymes, though, lack sufficient inventiveness or charm. The stances seem as indistinct as the rhyme of "lame" and "reign"; Foxy Brown neither vividly promotes herself nor undercuts her rival through pointed insult or inventive self-praise. The lines undercut their own assertions by promising a force they do not possess.

With her superior skills, Lil' Kim reasserts the status that Foxy Brown seeks. Both follow a hip-hop convention. In this kind of insult rhyme, the battle of rivals, participants face members of the same gender. Members of the opposite gender primarily appear as secondary targets: figures associated with the rival, but not significant in their own right. According to hip-hop's politics, the women remain gendered but the men do not. For this reason, a man always claims the honor of the best hip-hop artist. Playing by these rules in "Came Back for You," Lil' Kim groups Foxy Brown with another female challenger, Eve, in order to dismiss both: "So keep your tacky ways and go back to your stripper days/As long as I'm around, you gonna bow down."[38] Lil' Kim damns her rival with a rhyme both factual and malicious. (Eve admitted that she worked as a stripper before her hip-hop career developed.) Never known as a model of clean living or a wearer of tasteful attire, Lil' Kim recasts an insult often directed at her. Naming Lil' Kim Hollywood's second tackiest celebrity (a runner-up to Courtney Love), Fox News cited her outrageous behavior and outfits: "[W]hen you've had Diana Ross fondle you on stage, posed for album covers spread-eagle and in rock clown-makeup, you have taken the Tack to another level."[39] Lil' Kim's verse brushes aside such embarrassments. The basic rhyme of "ways" and "days" emphasizes the modifiers, presenting Eve as not only a "stripper" but also a "tacky" one. The double-edged rhymes condemn Eve to her sordid past while, stylish and sly, they elevate Lil' Kim as the embodiment of good taste.

Lil' Kim wins the insult battle because she presents a superior self-mythology. Her verse exemplifies the greatness she claims, striking a balance of menace and self-praise. She moves easily between the two modes, because each supports the other:

> It's the real hip hop. Mami, check the facts.
> I'm sick of all you acts with your bubble gum raps.

Like the sand in the hourglass you out of your time.
Try to go against the queen is you out of your mind?
("CBFY")

Lil' Kim presents herself as the true "mami," the top female.
To claim this status, she wittily erases one rival's name from
the Bible. "Kim" replaces "Eve," a mistake of creation, as the
first woman. Lil' Kim refuses to pronounce Foxy Brown's
self-aggrandizing stage name as if unwilling to validate the
flattery. Instead, she replaces "Foxy" with an image of gross
physicality, making her rival's name into an excremental
caricature:

Even be at number two, your chances is slim,
'cause when God made Adam, he should've made Kim.
I gave a few passes, but I never forget.
It's enough I got to put up with this Doo Doo Brown
chick. ("CBFY")

Finally referring to herself in the third person, Lil' Kim
simultaneously boasts and taunts:

I'm the best that ever done it, the best that lived it.
I ain't no overnight success. God damn it, I was born
with it,
the Prada mama, the Dolce and Gabbana drippin',
the Blue Hypnotic, Martini mimosa sippin'. ("CBFY")

The rhymes grow in complexity and frequency, offering
flourishes as extravagant as the luxuries she enjoys. The
opening presents a stark choice, reinforced with insistent
lines meant to intimidate. The final lines, though, charm.

The syntax turns elaborate and the references more allusive. The final two lines consist of names, of products rhymed into glamorous epithets. According to the song's own claim, its artistry reveals more than cleverness, hard work, or luck. "I ain't no overnight success," Lil' Kim announces: "God damn it, I was born with it." Born Kimberly Denise Jones, Lil' Kim presents self-creation as destiny. Adjusting the terms familiar to many fairy tales, she claims the name due her: a "queen" raised in humble obscurity. The swaggering final lines consist wholly of self-epithets pitched above the denigrations that she hurls at her rivals and against those that her rivals hurl at her, a seemingly eternal invective that continues as if by its own volition. They do more than rebuke pretenders. In the battle of names, Lil' Kim's rhymes establish her royalty.

Lil' Kim's "Came Back for You" shares the same basic structure as Jay-Z's smoother rhymes and the harsh attack that "Fuck tha Police" offers: each features a series of end-stopped couplets meant to be remembered. Hecht's grand vocabulary and serpentine syntax remain deliberately august, as if untempted by "Fortune, (our Eternal Whore)," but a similar organization animates his verse. In hip hop, this strategy favors a certain articulation. "I speak clearly so you can understand," Daddy Kane boasts while KRS-One notes clarity's professional benefits: "I speak clearly and that's merely/Or should I say a mere, help to my career."[40] Many hip-hop artists emerging in the 1980s favored this kind of rhyming. More recently, another mode has grown increasingly popular. The Wu-Tang Clan's appropriately titled "Triumph" exemplifies this approach. "I bomb atomi-cally. Socrates' philosophies/and hypotheses can't define how I be droppin' these/mockeries," Inspectah Deck announces before demonstrating what this kind of artistic success entails:

> lyrically perform armed robbery,
> flee with the lottery. Possibly they spotted me.
> Battle-scarred shogun, explosion when my pen hits,
> tremendous, ultra-violet shine blind forensics.[41]

The rhymes aim to overwhelm possible opponents. The first four lines, for instance, contain two rhyme groups: (1) "philosophies," "Socrates," "hypothesis," "droppin' these," and "mockeries"; (2) "atomically," "robbery," "lottery," and "spotted me." The first group off-rhymes with the second, presenting a total of nine instances in three lines. In the remarkable opening line, only two syllables do not rhyme, dominated by the eleven syllables that do. Multiple rhymes, Arthur Schopenhauer maintained, offer "an aesthetic neoplasm, a double coverage which is of no use."[42] According to him, a third rhyme forms a pair with the second but connects too distantly with the first, giving the impression of two pairs of rhymes, not three rhymes of the same sound. "Triumph" turns this confusion into a strength. Instead of crafting discreet couplets, this kind of hip hop values speed: metaphors that abruptly shift and rhyme schemes that gain velocity. Dominating each line, such rhymes bear a violent force. Each insists on the speaker's toughness and his eagerness to fight. Such quick rhymes leave little space for resistance; the listener strains to catch each one, let alone form a retort. The boast doubles as an insult. I can do this, the rhymes brag, and you cannot.

These hard rhymes boast of their power. Unironically, Inspectah Deck likens his rhymes to atom-bomb explosions and shotgun blasts, extending a well-established hip-hop tradition. "[T]his ain't a rap verse," Wyclef Jean declares. "It's more like a voodoo curse/So when you die kids'll throw rocks at ya hearse."[43] As represented in these lines, successful rhymes drive an opponent to the grave and haunt him beyond it. Hip hop presents this startling notion as ordinary; countless songs play variations on this commonplace. "I'm gonna curse you with lyrical voodoo," T-Pain maintains, literalizing Wyclef Jean's comparison: "My rhythms and rhymes keep niggas in line."[44] To express their rhymes' authority, Wu-Tang Clan introduces a series of metaphors, Wyclef Jean proposes a simile, and T-Pain offers a flat declaration. All, though, reject the notion that rhyme functions simply as a trope.

Hip-hop artists hold a different view of how poetic technique functions than do many scholars of contemporary poetry, who see rhyme as a fanciful gesture, a verse decoration, especially the kinds that many hip-hop songs favor: multisyllabic and mosaic rhymes, which print-based poets most commonly reserve for light verse. Many hip-hop artists see rhyme as possessing a fearsome authority, one that they eagerly claim. The technique represents more than a wish fulfillment or play acting. The rhyme completes the curse, enacting the desired result. In blunt terms, rhymes change lived reality.

In this respect, hip-hop artists are more traditional than nearly all contemporary poets and literary critics. In his book on Irish mythology, Yeats describes a mistreated traveler, a vagabond given bad lodgings. Enraged, he curses the friar whom he is told is responsible. Awakened by the noise, the friar, named Coarb, asks the lay brother what is happening:

> "It is a glee man," said the lay brother, "who complains of the sods, of the bread, of the water in the jug, of the foot-water, and of the blanket. And now he is singing a bard's curse upon you, O brother Coarb, and upon your father and your mother, and your grandfather and your grandmother, and upon all your relations."
>
> "Is he cursing in rhyme?"
>
> "He is cursing in rhyme, and with two assonances in every line of his curse."[45]

The friar and lay brother debate what they should do, concerned that the vagabond "will teach his curses to the children in the street, and the girls spinning at the doors, and to the robbers on the mountain of Gulben." The lay brother proposes that they should give him "a fresh loaf, clean water in a jug, clean foot-water, and a new blanket, and make him swear" not to share his rhymes. The friar rejects the idea, explaining:

> the next day the mood to curse would come upon him, or a pride in those rhymes would move him, and he would teach his lines to the children, and the girls, and the robbers. Or else he would tell another of his craft how he fared in the guest-house, and he in his turn would begin to curse, and my name would wither. (*M*, 150–151)

This possibility so terrifies the monks that they crucify him. Their fearful respect for rhyme's power sounded old-fashioned even to Yeats, one of the self-proclaimed "last romantics."[46] More than a century later, the literary culture has not revived it. Yet the wider society harbors a furtive concern that rhyme retains a certain malevolent influence, able to make consumers buy products they do not need and jurors set a killer free. The ancient fear survives as a modern suspicion. Using the resources of their time, hip-hop artists exploit this quiet apprehension with a confidence some might find exaggerated, if not ludicrous. Proud of their rhymes, the aggrieved curse so their adversaries' names wither.

MAKING LOVE IN MIRRORS

Hip-Hop Seduction Verse

IN THE OPENING OF NE-YO'S R&B song "Mirror," the speaker approaches his lover with a practiced air of bashful sincerity. "I must be honest with you babe," he repeats before he almost blushingly admits, "I love to watch the faces that you make (when we make love)." As if gaining courage but still apologetic, he explains:

> But when I'm behind you holding your hips
> and you close your eyes and bite your lips.
> I can't see you so might I suggest a change?
> Now mama please don't think me strange...

Encouraged, the speaker more boldly pleads:

> Baby I love making love in front of the mirror (in front of the mirror)
> So that I can watch you enjoying me (baby tonight)
> Baby tonight let's try in front of the mirror (in front of the mirror)
> Watching ourselves make love, girl why don't we...[1]

In technique and attitude, the song departs from the stock figure of the brash seducer, a role not unfamiliar to Ne-Yo. "I normally can talk a bum into buying dirt," another of his rhymes brags. "I normally can talk a nun up out of her skirt."[2] In contrast to the anonym rhyme of "bum" and "nun," the chorus uses one of the simplest rhymes in English, "we"/"me," a pair of plain, one-syllable pronouns differentiated by only a single letter, similar in sound, grammar, and semantic meaning. The rhyme strategically renounces any verbal trickery. In this respect, it resembles the speaker who presents himself as guilelessly sincere: "I must be honest with you babe (just gotta be honest babe)." Despite his hedging asides, he hardly suffers from debilitating shyness. To place a mirror before the lovers is to change the nature of their lovemaking. The mirror redefines the bodies and their actions. In contrast to the lover's presumably spontaneous gesture, "you close your eyes and bite your lips," the speaker wants to witness the effect his lovemaking achieves or, rather, he wants both lovers to watch each other and themselves. Changing pronouns, he urges his lover to open her eyes. "So that I can watch you enjoying me" turns into the mutual arousal of the two lovers "[w]atching ourselves make love."

Adjusting these strategies, lovers in hip-hop seduction songs perform for each other and themselves, as well as for a host of others: most often, sexual rivals. Intimate disclosure coexists with preening self-regard. Masters of the genre develop sophisticated, inventive forms in order to craft this boasting into a shared pleasure. At times the widely noticed misogyny and homophobia the songs voice remain obvious. The least attractive aspects, the repellent attitudes they occasionally express, obscure what is most vital and compelling. More strikingly, such gestures coexist with subtle overtures,

stylish effects, and schemes. Rhymes harness a range of energies. They couple bluntness and indirection, crassness and
resourcefulness, earthiness and refinement. A certain belief
animates the poetry: the confidence that rhyme serves as a
powerful tool for sexual enticement. In short, rhyme seduces.

To carry erotic power, words must embody desire's force,
not simply transcribe it. To demonstrate this principle, a
song may seduce even when its words seemingly describe a
hopelessly unsexy situation, as when the Pierces bemoan that
life has grown boring:

> Nothing thrills us anymore.
> No one kills us anymore.
> Life is such a chore
> when it's…boring.[3]

Consider the same stanza with the rhymes removed:

> Nothing thrills us.
> No one excites us any longer.
> Life is such a chore.
> when it's…dull.

As if cataloging an inventory, the original song itemizes the
objects of desire that have lost their power to excite. One
stanza, for instance, casts a hip-hop verse in miniature, presenting a list of fashionable luxury goods familiar to the
genre, slimmed to a skeletal rhyme, "Galliano/Donatella/
Dolce & Gabbana/Boring" ("B"). The hard-to-categorize,
folk-rock duo employs a hip-hop rhyming style. Yet the song
is hardly mournful, enervated, or chaste. In the song's video,
an Internet sensation, the two singers languidly vamp as

their voices stretch each syllable, lingering on the rhymes. Transcribed onto the page, the rhymes similarly invoke the pleasures that the singers intimately know and the listener seeks. Counterparts to the singers' vocal style and physical presence, the rhymes introduce a seductive presence, a sonic physicality. The rhymes recall their performers' attractive bodies. The rhymes excite and titillate; they coax eroticism from an unsexy vocabulary and syntax. The words confess a putative dullness, but the rhymes evoke sophisticated pleasures too carnal to name. They tease with a knowing wink; they flirt and entice. The revised lines sound plaintive and depressed, lacking style and energy. With the rhymes excised, only the boredom remains.

In much seduction verse, though, rhyme shifts emphasis from the given facts of the performers' bodies to their creative retelling. The goal is not truth telling but arousal, whether through flattery, humor, braggadocio, or a combination of these and other strategies. In "Work It," Missy Elliot encourages a potential lover:

> Boy, lift it up, let's make a toasta.
> Let's get drunk, it's gonna bring us closer.
> Don't I look like a Halle Berry poster?
> See the Belvedere playin' tricks on ya.[4]

Taking aim at these lines, Afroman scoffs, "Missy Elliot thinks she looks like Halle Berry/That scary," but his sneer deliberately misses the point.[5] He literalizes a provocative comparison in order to debunk it. Calculatingly and playfully, though, Missy Elliot exploits the difference between her actual appearance and the version that desire creates. Missy Elliot may have "[l]ost a few pounds" as a later line reports, but she hardly resembles "Halle Berry," let alone the starlet in airbrushed form. Nor she does pretend to. Instead, she announces that desire plays "tricks," welcomed ones, sophisticated and vulgar as a couple getting drunk on premium vodka.

Ne-Yo and Missy Elliot offer different figures for a similar effect. In Ne-Yo's version, the mirror changes the action it reflects. More an enticement than reportage, it makes sex even more desirable. Missy Elliot's "Belvedere" also transforms; it restyles the speaker, remaking an unremarkable body into a sexual ideal. Despite their differences, both songs share a particular logic familiar to much hip-hop seduction verse. Most commonly, the genre uses rhyme to achieve two specific effects. Rhyme establishes the seducer's sexual credentials. To rhyme well, wittily, inventively, and confidently is to promise sexual mastery. One skill confirms the other because rhyme embodies a carnal force. In this kind of seduction rhyming, the artists often craft flamboyantly elaborate structures, adding noticeable difficulties to rhyming in order to convey their erotic worth. Because rhyming skill equates with sexual prowess, they increase rhyming's challenges in order to prove their sexual fitness. The more difficult the rhyme, the more pleasures it promises. The second strategy stresses the atmosphere that rhyme establishes more than any virtuoso technique. Rhyme's ubiquity appears as inevitable as the proposed sexual consummation. As in insult verse, rhyme establishes a parallel relation between words and what they represent. While insults often use this parallelism in order to sharpen an opposition, seduction eroticizes the connection, presenting words powerfully drawn to each other. They charge the language with sexual potential. Used for this purpose, rhyme evokes physicality and sexual drive;

it stages "a copulation of sounds," as Octavio Paz describes the technique.[6] The patterns create a soundscape thick with innuendo and flirtation, with repeated consummation. As the rhymes embody sex, they insist on a particular logic: just to hear them to accept the seducer's advances.

These strategies and stances remain familiar enough for performers to play with and against them, sometimes within the same song. "Our rhyme's an aphrodisiac," Run-D.M.C. famously declared.[7] Appreciating this potential, hip-hop artists construct elaborate rhyming schemes and displays of formal skill designed to entice potential lovers. In this respect, their work resembles the most prestigious forms of contemporary poetry far less closely than those of Renaissance sonneters, the "active gallants" (as a sixteenth-century reader wrote) "devising how to win their Mistress' favours...blaze and blanch their passions, with aeglogues, Songs, and Sonnets, in pitiful verse."[8] Central to the lover's art, rhyming offered a crucial test. To develop this skill is to claim an important qualification. To fail to do so is to suffer a discrediting embarrassment. In *Much Ado about Nothing*, Benedick confirms this value system's currency when he laments how he cannot compose a successful love sonnet, despite his efforts:

> Marry, I cannot show it in rhyme. I have tried. I can find out no rhyme to 'lady' but 'baby', an innocent rhyme; for 'scorn' 'horn', a hard rhyme; for 'school' 'fool', a babbling rhyme. Very ominous endings. No, I was not born under a rhyming planet.[9]

As he admits, Benedick cannot master an apparently indispensable skill. Living in a sophisticated rhyming culture, he recognizes bad examples and their particular failures, their "innocent," "hard," and "babbling" qualities, but he cannot meet the standard. To borrow a phrase from *Henry V*, he envies "these fellows of infinite tongue, that can rhyme themselves into ladies' favours" (*TOS*, 623).

This ambition hardly inspires the most prestigious forms of modern and contemporary poetry and poetry criticism. It strikes many of the era's most celebrated poets and critics as (at best) quaint or (at worst) outmoded, offensive, or risible. "If Art were magic," scoffed W. H. Auden, "then love lyrics would be love charms which made the Cruel Fair one give one her latch key. In that case a magnum of champagne would be more artistic than a sonnet."[10] In contrast, hip hop delights in rhyme's ability to offer "love charms." They claim the opportunities and functions that the most prestigious forms of print-based poetry typically reject and respond to contemporary culture's insistent demands, the opportunities that its technologies and desires offer. If, as Marjorie Garber observes, the sonnet served as "the standard form of Elizabethan love-longing,"[11] hip hop provides many of its most forceful contemporary versions.

In their duet, "Promiscuous," Nelly Furtado and Timbaland exchange "love charms" in the form of rhymes. Through this technique, they test each other's sexual fitness. The ideas that the song expresses remain routine, but its rhymes cleverly entice. Starting a series of couplets and quatrains, Nelly Furtado, for instance, introduces a multisyllabic rhyme: "You expect me to just let you hit it/But will you still respect me if you get it?"[12] Accepting the invitation and the challenge, Timbaland responds with his own matching rhyme: "I'll be the first to admit it/I'm curious about you, you seem so innocent" ("P"). Because the rhyme serves as her main question, he answers it more than her actual query.

To add another rhyme is to show the "respect" she desires. "You wanna' get in my world, get lost in it," Nelly Furtado replies. "Boy, I'm tired of running, let's walk for a minute" ("P"). Like the drumbeat that drives the song's melody, the rhymes propel the lovers' words, guiding them to consummation. In this highly formulaic banter, they also hold the couple in check, allowing their anticipation and desire, their enjoyment, to build. The conventional nature of the exchange encourages the bantering humor, its mocking and heartening tone. The couple knows they perform expected roles; they aim to do so with style. Toward this goal, inventively they revise clichés. With mock weariness, Nelly Furtado exclaims, "Roses are red. Some diamonds are blue./Chivalry is dead, but you're still kinda cute" ("P"). Recasting the nursery rhyme, she switches "violets" to "diamonds," the seducer's lavish gifts, and abandons its concluding rhyme, as if settling for a less-than-perfect lover who is simply "kinda cute." The rhyme, though, offers him the opportunity to update this lost ideal. Recognizing the situation, Timbaland fills in the absent element, the expected compliment that she withheld. His next couplet rhymes with the missing word, "you": "Hey! I can't keep my mind off you/Where you at, do you mind if I come through?" Rhyming her desire with his, adroitly he shows his responsiveness, providing a contemporary version of the chivalry she wants.

Again, rhyme performs crucial functions. It confirms the couple's basic compatibility as one potential lover ends the other's rhyme. It allows each to display quick wit and savvy, mastery of the situation. Instead of presenting "eros as lack," the rhymes present erotic fulfillment as inevitable as their next iteration. They stage consummation: an excess, not a separation or shortage.[13] When the rhyme signals that the artists offer stylized versions of themselves, that is, when rhyme's mirror recasts them as ideals, paradoxically this self-aggrandizement more invites than excludes the listeners. The lovers present themselves as simultaneously exceptional and representative: an ideal and an everyman or every-woman. Reinforcing this dynamic, their boasting is meant to arouse their listeners as much as each other.

To this end, hip-hop seduction verse strives to be useful. "[T]he rhythm of the mix tape," the music critic Rob Sheffield observes, "is the rhythm of romance, the analog hum of a physical connection between two sloppy, human bodies."[14] Whether as a cassette, disc, audio file, or another format, the kind of mixtape that Sheffield describes—that is, a gift containing songs the lovers select and sequence—performs a wide range of precisely calibrated gestures. It might signal initial interest and deeper commitment, express desire, inten-sify love making, plead forgiveness, or lament a breakup. To achieve the desired end, mixtapes require a particular kind of expertise, as well as material. (A bad mixtape can produce disastrous results.) Hip-hop seduction verse remains attuned to these possibilities as the art adapts to new means of distri-bution, new expressions of desire. Contemporary lovers are much more likely to exchange mixtapes than love sonnets. "A great mix tape," as Sherman Alexie summarizes its happier effects, "[w]as sculpture designed to seduce."[15]

Exploiting hip-hop seduction verse's flexibility, its practi-tioners adjust its conventions to suit their temperaments and talents. When the Bloodhound Gang rhymes, "You and me baby ain't nothin' but mammals./So let's do it like they do on the Discovery Channel,"[16] the multisyllabic rhyme disarm-ingly sweetens the come-on. Most effectively, it evokes what is not. It recasts an animal drive into a playful act, offering self-deprecation, not braggadocio. While many hip-hop seduction songs detail the seducer's suave preparations, the rhyme pair evokes a decidedly gawky scene: a couple watching cable television's least erotic program. The technique eschews its customary coolness. Deliberately disengaging with hip-hop seduction verse's flashier conventions, it slyly turns a deficiency into an asset. The pick-up line teases its own ambition and the rhyme succeeds if the addressed woman laughs.

Of all the forms of hip-hop seduction verse, though, the subgenre in which the speaker seduces a rival's girlfriend or wife typically offers the most extravagant rhyming. "I gotta take you from your man," the subgenre's most fervent practitioner, LL Cool J, announces. "That's my mission./If his love is real he got to handle competition."[17] To accomplish and document this "mission," rhyme serves as both enticement and evidence of success. "I'm rhymin' and designin'," he boasts, "with your girl in my lap."[18] More elaborately, LL Cool J constructs another song, "Pink Cookies in a Plastic Bag Getting Crushed by Buildings," around a series of rhyming puns that the speaker exchanges with a potential lover:

> She said, "You tried to play me like Big Daddy."
> I said, "I know your Tribe, I Called and reQuested
> for you to be manifested."

Responding, the potential lover starts another round:

> She said, "You know the Same Gang and my Flava
> Unit too?"
> I said, "You only knew the certain things I wanna do,
> do you?

Rub ya down with warm Ice-T,
make ya feel Brand Nubian instantly.
Boogie Down and check this Production."[19]

The speaker and his beloved self-consciously perform conventional roles. Understanding what the other wants, each
demonstrates mastery of a familiar situation. When, for
instance, she complains with mock outrage, "You tried to
play me like Big Daddy," the challenge is clear. To gain her
affection, he must exceed Big Daddy Kane's performance and
"play" her with greater skill and deftness.

To prove his worth, LL Cool J updates a long history
of literary seduction, complete with particular stances and
strategies. Most conspicuously, he adds difficulties to the
couplet's demands. Over the course of the song, he mentions the names of thirty other hip-hop artists and groups.
In just the eight lines quoted above, for instance, he refers
to a half-dozen: Big Daddy Kane, A Tribe Called Quest,
Flavor Unit, the West Coast Rap All-Stars, Brand Nubian,
and Boogie Down Productions. Their sheer numbers pose
a formal challenge. To incorporate so many names requires
significant rhyming skill and attention.

Repeatedly LL Cool J names the figures of his moment,
the most accomplished hip-hop artists of the early 1990s,
craftily using them to his advantage. In her groundbreaking
study *Between Men, English Literature and Male Homosocial
Desire*, Eve Kosofsky Sedgwick described how frequently
and powerfully literature that expresses "male heterosexual
desire" involves erotic triangles between two male rivals and
a female beloved.[20] Drawing from the work of René Girard,
Sedgwick notes that "in any erotic rivalry, the bond that links
the two rivals is as intense and potent as the bond that links

either of the rivals to the beloved" (*BMEL*, 21). Reproducing this dynamic, LL Cool J attends more closely to his rivals than to his beloved. Instead of an erotic triangle, though, he presents a more populated situation: a metaphoric classroom that doubles as an execution chamber. "I'll take 30 electric chairs," he announces, "and put 'em in a classroom/30 MCs" ("Pink Cookies"). As the metaphor suggests, each mention of a name achieves multiple effects. To take attendance is also to execute a death sentence. Also, each time the speaker condemns a rival to the "electric chair," he gains a corresponding charge, an animating erotic current. The metaphor's fierceness, however, barely disguises the underlying affection. While LL Cool J contests a generation's top artists, he also pays homage to his favorites. In this respect, the seduction resembles a collaboration more than a competition. Describing how he likes to record songs with other performers, LL Cool J employs terms similar to those the song uses:

> I now really enjoy working with other artists. I love feeling their energy and their vibes and putting things together, then watching how it turns out....I learn things from other artists, too, all the time. I'll always be a student of hip hop.[21]

In "Pink Cookies," LL Cool J similarly acknowledges his influences, as well as his antagonisms. In his shifting terms, he remains a student as well as a teacher. He gains "energy." Presenting seduction as a shared art form, the roll call likewise invigorates the song as the rivals' very names turn into tools of enticement. Invoked in this fashion, his rivals offer a chorus of approval and encouragement.

In essence, the song balances two contrary energies. According to its violent central metaphor, the speaker proves

his worth by vanquishing all rivals. His rhyming skill condemns them and elevates him. At the same time, these
flourishes achieve a nonsensical charm. When the speaker
suggestively offers to "[r]ub ya down with warm Ice-T," the
come-on's particulars make little literal sense. Iced tea hardly
makes an enticing massage ointment. Its main logic is linguistic; the phrase contains a rival's name, the hip-hop artist
Ice-T. Like many of the others, the pun renounces menace
for a gentler appeal. At their most attractive, such gestures
offer a good-natured, almost goofy wink.

A pair of songs by Big Daddy Kane, one of LL Cool J's
formative influences, clarifies the strategies that LL Cool J
employs: what the potential lover means when she warns,
"You tried to play me like Big Daddy." In "Very Special," Big
Daddy Kane and Spinderella banter:

> "I talk the macho talk and keep my real feelings hidden."
> "But what about that 'Pimpin' Ain't Easy' stuff?"
> "Aw, I was just kiddin' cuz if we unite, baby, I'd do ya
> right."
> "Well, I hope you meant that mushy stuff you told Barry
> White."[22]

Hip-hop seduction verse forms a hybrid genre, adopting
stances and techniques taken from a host of available genres.
It potentially mixes, for instance, elements of gangsta rap,
soul, parody, pimp and dirty rap, as well as several others. In
this light comedy, Big Daddy Kane and Spinderella debate
their proper combination, their most attractive arrangement. In particular, she names two of Big Daddy Kane's
songs as potential models for his behavior: "Pimpin' Ain't
Easy" and "All of Me." The second reference requires a little

explanation. "All of Me" opens with another potential lover admitting, "Barry White, I love Barry White. He always puts me in the mood."[23] Sensitive to her preferences as well as the opportunities they present, the song turns into a duet, with Barry White encouraging Big Daddy Kane's amorous advances toward the woman. Addressing her, Big Daddy Kane admits, "I just wanna lay on the floor and make love to your shadow," before catching himself, "Sounds silly, don't it?" To which Barry White replies, reassuring him in the place of the potential lover, "Not really" ("AOM"). Big Daddy Kane remains aware of the situation's oddity. The song ostensibly enlists Barry White's assistance to seduce a woman but engages more with him than her. More neatly than LL Cool J's songs, it fits the triangular geometry that Sedgwick outlines. According to Spinderella, though, this arrangement exerts a useful influence, not homosocial exclusion. To this end, she encourages it. In her song's best line, she replies to his clichéd promise, "baby, I'd do ya right," "Well, I hope you meant that mushy stuff you told Barry White." Finishing Big Daddy Kane's rhyme, her flirtation takes the form of an insult. When he leaves it uncontested, Big Daddy Kane confirms they are not engaged in a battle rhyme, in which participants must address all slights, no matter how seemingly inconsequential. He recognizes her flirtatious tone. Spinderella wants a lover capable of both "macho stuff" and "mushy talk," a master of both modes. To fulfill this desire, Big Daddy Kane's opening declarations share the boastful syntax of "Pimpin' Ain't Easy," a first-person, two-verb line balanced with a midline pause, while expressing an idea quite foreign to that subgenre. The line's strength comes from its playful combination of toughness and sensitivity, its sense of restrained power. Accordingly Big Daddy Kane's generic versatility proves seductive. "Well, since you put it like that Daddy then we can do this" ("VS"), Spinderella concludes, finishing another of his rhymes.

Drawing from the same influence, Eminem characteristically pursues the opposite strategy. At nearly every moment in "Seduction," he proclaims his aggressiveness and dominance. Even more impressively, he claims this status by demonstrating a dazzling array of rhyming skills. After the introduction promises "a verbal seduction, seduction when I tell them girls on the floor,"[24] Eminem wastes little time in proclaiming his art's raw power. Rhyming transforms him, turning him into a stronger, more seductive version: "I feel like I'm morphing into something that's so incredible/That I'm dwarfing all competitors, better get your girlfriend in check" ("S"). The music provides the means for this "verbal seduction": not through tender promises and flattery, but through the rhymes' imposing force, their genius. "You better get a clue," early Eminem warns a rival with apparently vulgar directness:

> She's on my dick cause I spit better than you.
> What you expect her to do? How you expect her to act in the sack,
> When she's closing her eyes, fantasizing of
> Digging her nails in my back to this track? ("S")

A later verse returns to this idea, expressing it with a notably different rhyming technique:

> It's like we playing lyrical tug of war with your ear, you hear it? Girl, come here.
> Put your ear up to the speaker dear, while I freak this world premiere.

> Seducing her, loosen up with a little freestyle, better wait,
>   am I losing ya?
> Am I making you look bad? Well I got news for you,
>   homie, you're losing her. ("S")

These lines express a hip-hop commonplace with impressive skill. According to its familiar logic, the speaker claims the beloved from his rival because he possesses superior rhyming ability. In this "verbal seduction," the "ear" forms the truest body, the most contested and prized. To put this idea in slightly different terms, the ear represents the woman's most erotic and intimate organ. Adding an extreme illustration, the speaker possesses the beloved even at the very moment his rival has sex with her. The fantasy supersedes the situation's literal facts. To stress this point, Eminem mixes musical and bodily terms, emphasizing how his art reverses apparently abject sexual humiliation. When she is "digging her nails in my back to this track," his music, not his rival's body, brings her to sexual climax.

Vividly Eminem presents stances and ideas familiar to many hip-hop songs: "She might be with him/But she's thinkin' 'bout me, me, me,"[25] as Snoop Dogg puts it. With a nearly unparalleled technical artistry, though, Eminem's brooding rhymes prove the ideas they assert. The first passage features two sets of rhymes, the first consisting of three parts, "clue," "you," and "do," and the second consisting of four, "act," "sack," "back," and "track." Elegantly varying the syntax, he shifts blame from the desired woman to the rival. In the final line, the rhymes gain frequency and vehemence as the depicted act and the emotion it arouses gain intensity: "Digging her nails in my back to this track." This line combines a number of striking effects. The pronouns adjust across the line, "her," "my," and "this," staging a movement toward greater intimacy and connection, as the same song overwhelms both the speaker and the woman he desires. As the rhymes suggests, this process is neither gentle nor calm. Analyzing Yeats's line, "Stumbling upon the blood dark track once more," Richard Hugo observed that "the single-syllable word with a hard consonant ending is a unit of power in English, and that's one reason 'blood dark track' goes off like rifle shots."[26] Eminem's rhymes of "sack," "back" and "track" work similarly (in fact, they rhyme internally with Yeats's line and bear a similar metrical structure). Pairing single-syllable words with hard consonant endings, each presents a "unit of power." To adjust Hugo's simile, they explode across the line, urgent and punishing, tearing at what they desire.

Even more impressively, the second passage shifts to several distinctly different kinds of rhymes, stunning in their number and variety. In the first two lines, the dominant rhyme pattern claims at least seven examples:

> It's like we playing **lyr**ical tug of war with your **ear**, you **hear** it? Girl, come **here**.
> Put your **ear** up to the speak**er dear**, while I freak this world pre**miere**. ("S")

In a tour-de-force gesture, Eminem rhymes the opening syllable of "lyrical" with five one-syllable words, including a pair of homophones and the last syllable of "premiere." He also employs the one repeated rhyme word "ear," the passage's key word that evokes its argument: that the speaker appeals to the desired woman's "ear," the crucial part of her identity and sexual allegiance. A few numbers suggest some of the sheer technical variety at work. In just two lines, seven rhymes offer four kinds of rhyme: a one-syllable part of a multisyllabic word, several one-syllable words, a pair of homophones, and one repeated rhyme word. The movement from the start to the end of this line is particularly striking. The rhyme starts with the first syllable of a three-syllable word, "lyrical," then ends with the last syllable of a two-syllable word, "speaker." Not content with one word-splitting rhyme, Eminem adds another, rhyming the first syllable of "speaker" with "freak":

> It's like we playing lyrical tug of war with your ear, you hear it? Girl, come here.
> Put your ear up to the **speak**er dear, while I **freak** this world premiere. ("S")

In a kind of chiasmus rhyme, the first syllable of "speaker" introduces a new rhyme while the second syllable adds to the previous rhyme set.

Confirming Eminem's control and mastery, the last two lines work differently. In particular, they signal his considerable awareness of his art's history and development, his erudition. The final two lines include four multisyllabic rhymes, including a homophone and one repeated rhyme word, as well as a one-syllable rhyme, "news," that punctuates the pattern:

> Se**ducing** her, **loosen** up with a little freestyle, wait, am I **losing** ya?
> Am I making you look bad? Well I got **news** for you, homie, you're **losing** her. ("S")

In three instances, "Seducing her," "losing ya," and "losing her," pronunciation stretches the rhymes to three syllables.

This particular rhyming style achieves dual effects; it claims a particular lineage and distinguishes Eminem from less skillful rivals. In "Yellow Brick Road," Eminem offers a history of his artistic development. Faced with the challenge, "White boys don't know how to rhyme," he demonstrated his craft:

> I spit out a line and rhymed "birthday" with "first place"
> And we both had the same rhymes that sound alike.
> We was on the same shit, that Big Daddy Kane shit
> With compound syllables sound combined.[27]

A borrowed technique establishes Eminem's skill. To claim "first place," he follows Big Daddy Kane's innovation and crafts multisyllabic rhymes. To do so requires both critical discernment and artistic ability: alertness to his art's innovations coupled with technical expertise. This achievement stands apart from the particular emotion that the words express. Documenting his triumph, Eminem quotes only the rhyme words of his own depressive couplet: "I don't know why the fuck I'm here in the first place./My worst day on this earth was my first birthday."[28] The rhymes triumph even when the words express self-loathing despair. Later in "Seduction," the song returns to this particular kind of rhyme and the validation it brings. "I'm not about to sit back and just keep rhyming one syllable, nah," he explains. "Switch it up and watch them haters not give it up/Cause they're just not good enough but I'm not giving up" ("S"). Eminem's multisyllabic rhymes, his "compound syllables sound combined," distinguish him from less talented rivals. A subtle gesture particularizes the taunt. Punctuating the reference to those rivals who "keep rhyming one syllable, nah," he borrows

Jay-Z's manner of ending a line in order to mock him as "just not good enough."

To appreciate Eminem's rhymes, it is important to realize how they reverse the values of most prestigious forms of contemporary print-based poetry and poetry criticism. In particular, he prizes the kinds of rhymes that contemporary print-based poets generally avoid. In *Rhyme's Reason: A Guide to English Verse*, John Hollander cautions against two of the rhymes Eminem employs: "rhyming with too much more than one syllable" and homophone rhyme, "[t]he weakest way in which two words can chime."[29] Contemporary print-based poets also remain wary of rhymes that adjust a word's usual pronunciation in order to fit the pattern, a maneuver usually interpreted as indicating a lack of technical competence. In their glossary of literary terms, M.H. Abrams and Geoffrey Galt Harpham, for instance, describe "[t]his maltreatment of words, called forced rhyme, in which the poet gives the effect of seeming to surrender helplessly to the exigencies of a difficult rhyme."[30] Eminem's forced rhymes have the opposite effect. Instead of surrendering to difficulties, he dominates the language with his rhymes. It suggests skill and power, not ineptitude. As he brags elsewhere, "I just murdered the alphabet" ("Still").

Eminem offers virtually none of the seducer's classic overtures; he makes no attempt to anticipate his lover's wishes or enter a dialogue with her, whether fully staged or implied. For this reason, it is tempting to understand the song as a simple allegory. According to this interpretation, the woman represents hip hop. To claim her is to claim the art form. Eminem, perhaps the least romantic and fiercest hip-hop artist, also dramatizes the opposite idea. "Seduction" presents rhyme as essentially attractive. Powerful and brooding, it exposes performer and listener alike to a force larger than themselves, "morphing" them "into something that's so incredible." To borrow a term from Puttenham's *The Art of English Poesy*, his exceptional rhymes utter "amorous affections and allurements," almost regardless of what else they have to say.[31]

THE INHERITORS OF HIP HOP

Reclaiming Rhyme

THE JANUARY 3, 2011, EDITION of the *New Yorker* featured a poem by Kevin Young, the Atticus Haygood Professor of English and Creative Writing and the Curator of Literary Collections and Raymond Danowski Poetry Library at Emory University. "Expecting" describes two parents as their doctor performs a sonogram. After some anxious moments, the doctor finds the fetus's heartbeat, described as "all beat box and fuzzy feedback. You are like hearing/hip hop for the first time."[1] As Young's arresting simile suggests, a generation of print-based poets now coming into prominence claims hip hop as a resource. It serves as a shared experience and inspiration: more than aggravating background noise, what Rafael Campo calls the "blast/of hip-hop as some teenagers drive past," the urban landscape's "found rhythms,"[2] or the source of a few colorful slang terms. Instead, hip hop offers both material and artistic technique. Recent poems mention its performers and songs, anecdotes from the genre's development and the artists' lives. Epigraphs and titles quote songs.[3]

In interviews and in their verse, poets detail these formal choices, as well as the experiences that inspired them. "We studied master poets," announces John Murillo as if relating a generation's story, "Kane, not Keats;/Rakim, not Rilke. 'Raw,' ;I Ain't No Joke,'/Our Nightingales and Orpheus."[4] Another poem in the same collection, though, complicates this neat distinction. Murillo imagines a "pilgrimage" to Keats's grave, the fulfillment of "a poet's simple duty...To lay/Flowers on the graves of other poets" (*UJB*, 58). As this reverential gesture suggests, Murillo honors masters of both art forms: Kane *and* Keats, Rakim *and* Rilke. Sometimes, the results sound incongruous, if not jarring. "I wandered lonely as Jay-Z,"[5] Michael Robbins opens a poem, adding a favorite hip-hop performer to Wordsworth's canonical line. Asked about this coupling, Robbins described the two artists' similar "impact" on him:

> I make the obvious distinction between Wordsworth and Jay-Z, but I don't make a distinction in the impact they've had on my life. Each of them has provided me with what Kenneth Burke calls "equipment for living."[6]

As Robbins's comments suggest, one need not confuse Wordsworth with Jay-Z in order to value both. Instead, like many of his contemporaries, Robbins acknowledges the different resources that print-based poetry and hip hop provide, and he draws from both traditions.

While the various poets differ in emphasis and approach, a few general tendencies should be acknowledged. First, they typically share a certain generational experience. With a few exceptions, most notably Harryette Mullen (born in 1953) and D. A. Powell (b. 1963), the poets who most compellingly draw from hip hop, including Murillo (b. 1971), Major Jackson (b. 1968), Kevin Young (b. 1970), Terrance Hayes (b.

1971), Matthew Dickman (b. 1975), and Erica Dawson (b. 1979), started listening to music during the 1980s and 1990s, the era often defined as hip hop's "golden age," and its immediate aftermath, as landmark works such as Grandmaster Flash and the Furious Five's *The Message* (released in 1982), Run-D.M.C.'s *King of Rock* (1985), and Public Enemy's *It Takes a Nation to Hold Us Back* (1988) circulated through the culture. "Rap and I grew up together," Young relates. "[W]e are almost exactly the same age."[7] Drawn to the new form, Young was a DJ on his college radio station. Others wrote and performed their own lyrics; several simply listened to the music with keen appreciation. "Rap was the first music I really understood," notes Adrian Matejka, "and it seemed like it was made for me."[8] This intimate connection marks these poets' growing awareness of themselves as artists. The music formed a significant part of their artistic identity and training. More than a childhood amusement, hip hop proved useful, suggesting alternatives to entrenched tendencies in print-based poetry and offering techniques and stances to address the challenge that, for better or worse, concerns much recent American poetry: the need to sound contemporary.

Another recent poem about hip hop clarifies these strategies. The title poem of Matthew Dickman's celebrated debut collection, *All-American Poem*, issues an invitation that doubles as a young poet's swaggering self-presentation. Tellingly, the poem's first word is "I":

> I want to peel off a hundred dollar bill
> and slap it down on the counter.
> You can pick out a dress. I'll pick out a tie: polka dots
> spinning like disco balls. Darling let's go
> two-stepping in the sawdust at the Broken Spoke.

Let's live downtown and go clubbing.
God save hip-hop and famous mixed drinks.[9]

Other poems in the collection praise the music with greater specificity. Borrowing the title of Jay-Z's album, "The Black Album" describes "the world coming together, crashing/ around us, while we drive through the forests of Vermont,/ listening to *The Black Album*, blasting it," an experience likened to "the way you feel when you're moving/along like a train running, furious" (*AAP*, 20).

Both Dickman and Young borrow the conventions of earlier poems about American popular music, but they recast their associations. They not only update the reference but also update the intended effect. Instead of rock and roll, they mention hip hop, but more important, the music conveys a different force. Exemplifying these earlier poems, Campbell McGrath's "Guns N Roses" praises the band's heavy metal anthem "Sweet Child o' Mine" as the expression of a generation's experience. The song's most powerful sections, the poem relays, "sound like how it felt to be alive/at that instant."[10] With a tone both ecstatic and mournful, the poem elegizes the late 1980s and a friend who shared that era. Dedicated to "I. M. TIM DWIGHT, 1958–1984," the poem memorializes a double loss, personal and cultural. At the same time, the poem's breakneck style imitates the song's force: "embodying everything rock and roll aspires to be,/heroic and violent and joyous and juvenile/ and throbbing with self-importance" (*PA*, 48). The sprawling long-lined free verse claims a rock-and-roll style, tempered with a sense of diminishment: literary self-consciousness and middle-aged regret.

Written by an author born in 1962 and published in 2004, "Sweet Child o' Mine" is a Baby Boomer rock-and-roll poem par excellence. With great panache, it follows a recognizable formula. "Baby Boomers who published books of poems after the 1960s used rock," Stephen Burt notes,

> to invoke youth, rawness, energy, spontaneity, sex—all the supposedly adolescent qualities they could not claim for poetry itself. They wrote about rock when they wanted to think about the youth they felt they had lost, about its lost innocence or its failed revolutions.[11]

Such poetry assumes a number of distinctions: between music and poetry, rock's power and poetry's powerlessness, innocence and experience, youthful excitement and middle-aged regret. In Baby Boomer poetry, the music reinforces these divisions. When Boomer poets use rock and roll to "invoke" "all the supposedly adolescent qualities they couldn't claim for poetry itself," they contrast their art with the music, often to highlight poetry's disadvantages. Print-based poets influenced by hip hop often use the music to different effect; they reconfigure the relation of music and print-based poetry. To recast Burt's terms, they claim hip hop's qualities for their art. Instead of returning to a customary sense of failure and loss, the long sigh of much Boomer poetry, they find a useful model of expansiveness and promise.

Concerned with familial obligations, Young's "Expecting" remains closest to Baby Boomer poetry. It features a married couple, not a young man on the prowl, and a far less sexy and fashionable setting than a night club: an obstetrician's office. The trope of hip hop, though, lightens its apprehension. Hip hop replaces familiar world-weariness. It adds liveliness, the electricity of the moment, and a sense of potential: what Young calls "all promise" ("E," 43). As hip hop enters the poem, the language turns fanciful and less cautious, even when expressing a parent's fears. A celebration of possibility, it functions as a simile generator, a counterbalance to solemnity and linguistic restraint.

Like "Expecting," Dickman's poems would never be confused with actual hip-hop lyrics. "The Black Album" conspicuously differs from the song closest to it, "Allure," featured in the album that the title names:

> I never felt more alive than ridin' shotgun
> in Klein's green 5 until the cops pulled guns
> and I tried to smoke weed to give me the fix I need.[12]

The striking differences in setting, tone, language, and subject emphasize Dickman's use of hip hop as a trope, not a technical model. The scene that the poem "The Black Album" describes, a car ride in rural Vermont, could not differ more dramatically from the experience the song "Allure" recounts: working with a notorious drug dealer nicknamed Calvin Klein. Just as a bucolic setting, "the forests of Vermont," reinforces a racial difference, the phrase's slightly archaic syntax distances the poem from Jay-Z's street slang. In short, Dickman writes a poem that emulates the experiences of listening to hip hop, not, in a stricter sense, a "hip-hop poem."

In the context of print-based literary history, the driving excitement of Dickman's poetry departs from a more austere aesthetic. As with the earlier poems influenced by rock and roll, music suggests an alternative model to a late modernist poetics. "The compression of Pound's Imagist poems," James Longenbach observes, "has in many ways determined the direction of poetry in our language for the last hundred years. Most crucially, Imagism quickly became a limitation."[13]

Instead of "shrinking lyric utterance to its pithiest core" (as Longenbach describes late Imagist verse), Matthew Dickman writes expansively. Noisily his poems speed forward. They mix the retro and the new, the formal and the slangy. They present a staged spontaneity, an openness to whatever comes next. In one respect, the midcentury poets of the New York School offer an important model, but with an important difference. In his famous reading of the canonical poem of the New York School, Frank O'Hara's "The Day Lady Died," Andrew Ross notices:

> By 1959, the rock and roll revolution was over three years old, but you can comb through O'Hara's entire oeuvre—compendiously packed with cultural details—and never find any evidence that such a revolution had taken whole regions and sectors of the culture by storm.[14]

O'Hara's avoidance of rock music extended to his personal life. He did not listen to the music, let alone enjoy it. Adding a personal recollection, Joe LeSueur mentions the shock of hearing "music from the radio—*popular* music, which Frank never played" when he arrived at the apartment they shared, a sure sign that someone else was inside.[15] In Dickman's poems, popular music is always playing. Like O'Hara, he packs his poems with cultural details but takes popular music as both a trope and an inspiration. In Baby Boomer poems, rock and roll typically marks what the speaker has lost. Hip hop encourages Dickman to achieve a different effect. As the collection's title announces, his "All-American Poem[s]" see how much they can include, as if their aim were to travel the entire country. The poems gobble up language and culture and travel linguistic and musical geographies. Just as one line in another poem praises "Johnny Cash, Biggie Smalls, Johann Sebastian Bach" (*AAP*, 16), "The Black Album" shows how much meaning and poetic opportunity a single one-syllable word generates, riffing on it more than twenty times.

Tellingly, that word is "black." If hip hop offers Dickman a model of expansiveness, it also highlights a racial tension: in particular, the contentious issue of hip hop's white listenership. "White consumption of hip hop," charges Tricia Rose, "has a strong likelihood of reproducing the long and ugly history of racial tourism."[16] In Rose's formulation, race trumps all other considerations. Instead of transforming lived experience, the music most commonly reproduces a racial divide. In style and argument Dickman defends his enthusiasm, adding the sometimes overlooked category of class. "For music and poverty are the great regulators in the world," he observes, illustrating the point:

> when white kids in Kansas are bumping Tupac
> from the windows of Ford pickups, working
> in the canneries, dreaming of LA: raving and mad
> between turntables. (*AAP*, 19)

These lines contrast with another poem's description of other "white kids" defined by different music tastes; "white kids" who "listened to Black Sabbath/while they beat the shit out of each other/for bragging rights" (*AAP*, 58). In Dickman's terms, the music regulates their lives differently. Played by an all-white band, the heavy metal reinforces the teens' joyless isolation. The language remains flat and nearly monosyllabic, as defeated as the teens they describe, regardless of their fights' outcome. As in the cliché, "they beat the shit out of each other," each sinks to the status of human waste. The other description of "white kids" works differently. Enjambments speed the poem from Kansas to Los Angeles, from the white working poor to a dead hip-hop legend, the son of a Black Panther. The language likewise suggests the imagination's mobility. Borrowing slang from hip hop, the teens are "bumping Tupac," playing the car stereo at high volume. Sympathetically Dickman presents these often-disparaged figures, white consumers of hip hop, blasting their music for all to hear. Just as they are moving in their cars, the music propels them beyond their surroundings. More than "racial tourism," it enlarges their lives.

As described in the poem, hip hop inspires a sense of speed and propulsion, qualities that Dickman's poems also seek to capture. Even the speaker's tie, "polka dots/spinning like disco balls," cannot keep still. While Dickman's poems do not rhyme, other print-based poets explore hip-hop rhyming styles in their work. Their rhymes aim for a similar effect; "let's go," they command poet and reader alike.

Consider, for instance, the following stanzas:

Darryl Dawkins wrote a book,
And I might too. He liked the rhymes'
(*If you ain't groovin'*) paradigms
(*You best get movin'*). Hook

A chorus and we've got
A song, a stereo type, a *lieu*
De mémoire with a residue
Of minstrelsy: a forgot-

> Me-not like an earworm, like
> The scar telling a Frankenstein-
> esque tale on Dad's left heel, like fine
> Fixed fantasies. They psych…[17]

Erica Dawson's "Chocolate Thunder" gets as much as possible into its rhymes: to chart only a partial catalogue, it couples English and French, parts of words and whole words, basketball nicknames and literary-critical terms, visual opposites ("Frankenstein" and "fine"), semantic near-opposites ("got" and "forgot"), and multisyllabic and one-syllable words. As if the formal challenges that the envelope rhyme pose were not enough, the poem adds more. The third and fourth lines add an internal rhyme ("*groovin*"/"*movin*") to the end rhyme, so that the quatrain contains six rhyming words. To account for this variety, the poem proposes metaphor after metaphor for its handling of form: at times athletic, at times musical, and at times linguistic, "logogriph" (*BEA*, 31).

Dawson's *Big-Eyed Afraid* contains nine poems that fill twenty-five pages written in this style. All start with the phrase "I was born" or a close variation of it. Paradoxically, the phrase suggests the multitude of stories and identities the speaker inherits, revises, and recreates, the histories she is given and claims. Their titles suggest the wide range of identities they investigate: "Nappyhead," "Doll Baby," "Mommy Dearest," "God Girl," "White Dwarf," "Rikki-Tikki-Tavi," and "DrugFace." Individual poems add many, many more. "White Dwarf," for instance, mentions five in fewer than three lines: "Drama Queen," "Cow," "Diana Ross," "Wise Man," and "La Sexpot" (*BEA*, 29). The identities range from the ugly and the beautiful, the pious and the raunchy, the racially specific and the cross-racial, the glamorous and embarrassing. By retelling so many stories about herself, the speaker reveals how little she remains beholden to any one account. "[N]icknames," Ralph Ellison observed, "are indicative of a change from a given to an achieved identity."[18] To revise this formula, the poem delights in its powers of reinvention; it refuses to settle for a single "achieved identity." It adds nickname to nickname, asserting that the given facts of one's life matter less than their retelling.

Reinforcing this claim, "Chocolate Thunder" pays tribute to Darryl Dawkins. Dawkins was not the greatest basketball player of his era; he was, however, the most flamboyant. Beloved by hip-hip artists, he drew their praise as a model for their art. "Strong Like Chocolate Thunder," Kurtis Blow boasted, "[t]hat's the rhythm of the beat," while Ice Cube similarly bragged, "I rock a motherfuckin' mic 'til the break of day/Darryl Dawkins flow."[19] A prodigy who went straight from high school to the National Basketball League, Dawkins cultivated a reputation for grand eccentricity. As part of this effort, he claimed to be from Planet Lovetron because, as he explained, "I had too much funk to be tied down to one hometown."[20] Dawson's poem refers to Dawkins's memoir, which also takes its title from Dawkins's best-known nickname—famous enough for President Obama to greet the retired player when they met, "Chocolate Thunder!" ("Yessir, Mr. President," responded Dawkins.)[21]

Two moments in particular, though, define Dawkins's career. Twice he dunked the basketball with such ferocity that he shattered the backboards, then celebrated the dunks with elaborate rhyming names he crafted for them. In the memoir, Dawkins relates how he explained his first backboard-destroying dunk to reporters with his characteristic style:

> "I didn't mean to destroy it [the backboard]," I told sportswrit-ers after the game. "It was the power, the Chocolate Thunder. I could feel it surging through my body, fighting to get out. I had no control."
>
> I wound up calling my most famous dunk "If You Ain't Groovin' Best Get Movin'- Chocolate Thunder Flyin'- Robinzine Cryin'- Teeth Shakin'- Glass Breakin'- Rump Roastin'- Bun Toastin'- Glass Still Flyn'- Wham-Bam-I-Am-Jam!"[22]

Dawkins played a team sport, basketball, but his most famous exploits defy the activity's collective nature. Like Dawson's rhymes, his elaborate dunks added an apparently unnecessary difficulty. He concentrated on what some observers decried as a distraction. Speaking in general about the sport, the coach John Wooden, for instance, criticized what he called "the dunk" because "I think it's primarily showmanship," opposed to the shared aim: an "absolute stress on team play" (*WIWC*, 200). Gleefully Dawkins's actions celebrated the qualities Wooden dismissed. When Dawkins broke a backboard, that feat did not help his 76ers to win; it disrupted and nearly ended the game. Redefining the terms of the contest, the moment overwhelmed its putative occasion. The image of the backboard glass falling in shards achieved a status lost to that otherwise forgettable game. Decades later the clip continues to be replayed as a highlight. Dawkins's athletic style matched that of his versifying. Funny, funky, and profane, his rhymes celebrate a triumph of individual style, an assertion of his own amazing strength. As his memoir's subtitle proudly asserts, on and off the court he remained a self-avowed "showman."[23]

In "Chocolate Thunder," Dawson weds these qualities to an apparently unlikely form. In the poem, Daryl Dawkins meets Tennyson, the Victorian Poet Laureate. Like several other poems in her debut collection *Big-Eyed Afraid*, "Chocolate Thunder" reworks the "In Memoriam" stanza, a quatrain that features envelope rhyme, meaning that the first and fourth lines rhyme and the second and third lines rhyme. Dawson dramatically revises the form's associations, its apparently given identity. Discussing Tennyson's handling of stanzaic form in "In Memoriam" shortly after the work's publication Charles Kingsley observed:

> [T]heir metre, so exquisitely chosen, that while the major rhyme in the second and third lines of each stanza gives the solidity and self-restraint required by such deep themes, the mournful minor rhyme of each first and fourth line always leads the ear to expect something beyond.[24]

Following Kingsley's "most perceptive comment," subsequent generations of scholars emphasize how the stanza "rises" "and then fades" "into dimness and regret."[25] George Saintsbury, for instance, asserted that the connection between form and theme remained indisputable. "Once more, the fact is the fact," he flatly insists, noting the stanza's suitability for "pensive mediation." "I defy any one to use the *In Memoriam* stanza," he grandly concluded, "without dropping into such a vein, unless he is contented with simple burlesque, or likes to have his metre perpetually jostling his thought, like two ill-matched walkers arm-in-arm."[26] Describing Tennyson's versification, the scholars name the very qualities that Dawson avoids. Pursuing an alternative notion of rhyme, she accepts Saintsbury's challenge. Unlike Tennyson's, her rhymes cut across words and stanzas: "Franken*stein*-/esque" and the triple rhyme of "fine" and "got" and "for*got*-//me-*not*" (my italics). She seeks new rhymes and ways of rhyming. Instead of "solidity and self-restraint," the stanza pursues the possibilities its daring creates. Sometimes, the effect is a "Frankensteinesque" cobbling together of parts, ungainly and almost freakish. Delighting in their brawny speed, though, the rhymes aim for more than "simple burlesque"; they prize a funky showmanship. The lines that claim Dawkins as a model suggest how "[h]e liked the rhymes'/(*If you ain't groovin'*) paradigms/(*You best get movin'*)." The "rhymes"/"paradigms" possess a double meaning: the particular formal demands, meaning the specific versification scheme, and the broader imperative to move, either in delight or fear.

At its most successful, poetry that follows this aesthetic achieves a thrilling quality—stylish, daring, and excited. Each rhyme offers a kind of contest, seeing how much it can introduce and how far it can extend. It more stretches expectation than fulfills it. "I do think its [rap's] rhythms and rhymes have influenced my poetry," Dawson notes, explaining her method:

> I try to do something surprising, or inventive, with rhyme in my work. I try to rhyme words that you wouldn't expect to rhyme. I try to rhyme monosyllabic words with polysyllabic words. I try to create a way for rhyme to weave its way in and out of the rhythm so the reader/listener can be caught off-guard, hearing a rhyme in an unexpected place. There, then, is a sense of rhythm beneath the rhythm.[27]

This otherwise unobjectionable commitment to the "surprising, or inventive" rhyme, to catching the "reader/listener" "offguard" introduces a certain hazard. In its exuberant commitment to finding nearly whatever it can rhyme, it risks producing the verse equivalent of what the critic James Woods descries as the contemporary novel's "hysterical realism":

> The big contemporary novel is a perpetual-motion machine that appears to have been embarrassed into velocity. It seems to want to abolish stillness, as if ashamed of silence. Stories and substories sprout on every page, and these novels continually flourish their glamorous congestion.[28]

In the poetic version of this "glamorous congestion," rhymes, subrhymes, and allusions drive the work. They aim for spectacular displays. At times, rhymes proliferate with an almost overwhelming force as they seek rapidity and excitement. The resulting poems nearly burst with a self-involved need for more.

In *Alien vs. Predator*, Michael Robbins extends this principle to the breaking point. Whereas Dawson's poems pursue an energetic movement, compared to Robbins's they seem almost tranquil. When the speaker of Robbins's poem, "Human Wishes" exclaims, "Last night a DJ almost killed me./I'm as alive as you can possibly get" (*AVP*, 58), the lines yoke contraries in punning, self-referential language. To do so, they feast on slang and verbal culture, high and low. Most obviously, the lines reverse Indeep's "Last Night a DJ Saved My Life," which praises music's power to "send trouble down the drain."[29] Robbins's poem both resists and expands on this idea. To "kill me" could mean to murder or its opposite, to feel fully alive; that is, the first line could mean that a DJ almost murdered the speaker, beat him in a DJ battle, or that he overwhelmed the speaker with his own skill's power and, by doing so, allowed the speaker to feel exhilarated.

Like nearly all the poems in the collection, "Human Wishes" ends with a flourish. To be more precise, the poem consists of a series of flourishes:

> I never promised you a unicorn.
> But still. What is it like to be at bat?
> Just having *T.M.I.* tattooed on my balls.
> The heavy lice that hang from them
> run in blood down palace walls. (*AVP*, 58)

In this passage, allusions perform the function of the more extravagant rhyming that Robbins's work typically favors. Lines earlier in "Human Wishes," for instance, couple the demotic and hermeneutic: "the Bible says, *Shawty you must get loose*" and "Its exegesis is abstruse" (*AVP*, 58). While this passage offers a rather plain rhyme, "balls" and "walls," its allusions offer a corresponding busyness.

To suggest the range of the references, it is important to name their sources before grappling with the broader question of their purpose. This allusion hunting might seem a peculiarly academic exercise, except for the fact that the contemporary artists most likely to inspire it are hip-hop performers, who offer allusions at such a dizzying pace that several websites have arisen to help listeners discern them. "Rap Genius," for instance, glosses lines in order to "critique rap as poetry." Insightful comments allow contributors to "earn Rap IQ™."[30] Demonstrating the density of an apparently straightforward line, the website lists three possible interpretations for Drake's simile, "Like we sittin' on the bench, nigga, we don't really play."[31] In interviews downloaded onto the website, a number of performers participate in this process, recognizing that it celebrates their artistry. Particularly prized is an artist's ability to carry multiple meanings across phrases, whether through homophones, puns, or other devices. Double entendres earn praise for their inventiveness, style, and originality. "[D]oubling up," a columnist for Rap Genius concludes, "is the hallmark of a clever rapper."[32]

Robbins's references pursue a more jittery movement; they pinball between different concerns instead of enacting simultaneous multiple meanings. Hiply they mix the cool and uncool, creating a funhouse mirror of contorted references. The passage's opening line, for instance, recasts a cultural cliché, a phrase quoted and requoted for more than four decades with various degrees of sincerity and irony. It rhymes with the title of Joanne Greenberg's novel *I Never Promised You a Rose Garden*, the song written by Joe South and most famously recorded by Lynn Anderson, and the movie based on the novel. The line recalls a rather odd history, as a depiction of teenage schizophrenia inspired a romantic, uplifting country song. As if underscoring this disorienting descent into bad taste, the poem recasts a romantic cliché, a rose garden, into a wholly mythic creature, a "unicorn." The ghost rhyme makes the line sound even kitschier.

In contrast the second line truncates a much more august text: the philosopher Thomas Nagel's landmark essay "What Is It Like to Be a Bat?" In an interview, Robbins glosses the reference, "The bat, since Thomas Nagel's 'What Is It Like to Be a Bat?', is a metonym for what reductionist accounts of consciousness cannot conceive—the subjective character of experience, for instance" ("MR"). As the example of the bat suggests, one species cannot understand another's consciousness, despite its efforts to do so. "I want to know what it is like for a *bat* to be a bat," Nagel writes. "Yet if I try to imagine this, I am restricted to the resources of my own mind, and those resources are inadequate to the task."[33] Partly inspired by Nagel's essay, the bat serves as a motif in Robbins's poetry. Appearing in several poems, it suggests sympathy's limits, our restricted capacity to understand another's perspective, whether human or animal. With this emphasis on the mind's restrictions, Robbins's poem opposes Richard Wilbur's well-anthologized poem "Mind," often cited as a model of midcentury metaphysical verse, which elegantly delights in the powers that "Human Wishes" presents as inadequate. "The mind is like a bat. Precisely," Wilbur's poem concludes before revising the statement, "Save/That in the very happiest intellection/A graceful error may correct the cave."[34] In Wilbur's poems, the bat represents the mind's ability to transcend its apparent limits. In Robbins's evocation of Nagel's essay, the animal suggests how little the mind can know. Blurring the reference, Robbins revises the noun into a slang verb, "at bat," combining modes of intellect and action.

Finally the last line offers the passage's closest example to a hip-hop "doubling up," drawing from one of the most recognizable lines in English lyric poetry: namely, the close of William Blake's "London." Borrowing one line and one image from Blake, Robbins's poem literalizes the venereal disease that "plagues the Marriage hearse," but the speaker suffers it alone. Deflating Blake's social and prophetic vision, Robbins offers a speaker focused on his genitals. The reference to "balls" encourages the reader to recall the previous lines and recognize how similar imagery dominates them. In blunt terms, it compels the reader to realize how much the speaker has been talking about his (apparently diseased) penis. In the place of Blake's moral outrage, Robbins offers a gross-out joke.

Robbins's allusive style, though, most often returns to its antagonisms. Demonstrating this principle, the poem borrows its title from Robert Hass's collection, *Human Wishes,* an otherwise surprising choice given the fact that Robbins witheringly reviewed Hass's *The Apple Trees at Olema: New and Selected Poems*, which included selections from the earlier collection. Surveying Hass's work, Robbins objected to "the dewy piety that makes it impossible to read many Hass poems with a straight face," noting "the poet is so enamored of himself and his sincerity that he is rendered quite tone-deaf to the comic pseudo-profundity of his lines."[35] According to Robbins, the status Hass enjoys confirms that the literary culture values the wrong poetic qualities. Hammering at this point, the review repeatedly decries Hass's undeserved career and reputation. "Hass has made a career out of flattering middlebrow sensibilities with cheap mystery," Robbins asserts before bitingly concluding, "Hass has for years enjoyed a reputation that is disproportionate to his admirable but uneven powers probably because his work answers to a silly notion of poetry as a striving toward purity" ("AYS," 466–467, 470). Assiduously Robbins's verse avoids the "dewy piety" and "sincerity" that he perceives in Hass's poetry. He parodies Hass's lines that his review criticizes as risible. For example, he transforms Hass's declaration, "I/made a solemn face/and tried the almost human wail/of owls…/My wife stirred in our bed" into "My wife is asleep./I hoot like an owl into her hair.//That was a joke, by the way" (quoted in "AYS," 466; *AVP*, 58). He replaces Hass's "human wishes" with his own, draining them of solemnity, self-professed or not.

While Dawson's work playfully explores the question of how a self accepts and remakes the identities assigned it, Robbins constructs a poetics of deliberate, stagey vulgarity.

With little recourse to discredited notions such as "sincerity" or "piety," his poetry remains most alert to what it is not. In an age of Google, it would be unfair to call his references obscure. They do, however, lack certain satisfactions. Less clever than the hip-hop lyrics they evoke, they remain too impatient to develop their in-jokes into wit. Instead, harmlessly they circle rather small antagonisms.

Suggesting the diverse resources that hip hop offers contemporary print-based poets, Major Jackson draws from many of the same artists as Robbins, but to very different effect. Jackson presents poetry and poetic technique as models of cooperation, not antagonism. In this respect, hip hop forms a crucial example. Elaborating on this connection between artistic technique and historical imperative, the section of the sequence "Letter to Brooks" titled "Erie" opens with a declaration of artistic principles:

> I put a premium on rhymes—how could I
>   Not living the times of the Supa
> Emcees where styles are def, lyrics fly,
>   Tight the way our minds move over
>   Beats and grooves. Our brain matter's
> Amped, mic-checked so we non-stop.
> My spirit feels echoes thanks to hip hop.[36]

Rhyme performs a double function. It expresses the contemporary moment: "the times of the Supa/Emcees" in which the speaker lives. To rhyme is to respond to these imperatives; to appreciate the technique is to appreciate our moment. Accordingly, the poem draws rhyme words from contemporary idiom, signaling its assent: "Supa," "over" and "matter," and "non-stop" and "hip hop." More conspicuously, the next section rhymes "2Pac" and "fact" and the seventh section consists almost wholly of performers' names. Yet the rhymes also adhere to a specific pattern, one that originates from outside hip hop and significantly predates it. Jackson borrows the rhyme royal stanza that W. H. Auden employs in his "Letter to Lord Byron": "a form," as Auden characterized it, "that's large enough to swim in,/And talk on any subject that I choose."[37] Rhyme royal offers more than the specific pattern of ababbcc rhyme. "I feel Audenesque," (*H*, 58) Jackson playfully exclaims, acknowledging his borrowings.[38] Like Auden, Jackson uses this form for the expansiveness it encourages: the wandering mode capable of considering "any subject" the poet cares to address. In this respect, the poem's discursive style, its Audenesque emphasis on "talk," differs from the styles hip hop typically favors. In the poem's own terms, the "epistolary chat" (*H*, 57) remains open to hip-hop rhymes but also registers a certain distance.

As the poem asserts, though, to rhyme is to create "echoes," both aural and associative. Art trains its listeners to appreciate sometimes surprising connections, to hear and acknowledge them. " 'All real living is meeting,' " a poem later in the sequence quotes Martin Buber before adding, "we consent/To the same encounter reading lyrics" (*H*, 117). Jackson's personal experience taught him a similar lesson. Before either achieved their current stature, Jackson performed with the Roots (then called the Square Roots) at the Painted Bride Art Center, where he worked. A few years later, writing the liner notes for the group's album *Do You Want More?!!!??!*, Jackson explained "the genius of The Roots": "The Roots have a genius for building a community" before adding a telling qualification, "I guess good art does this."[39] "Good art," then, does not aim for idiosyncrasy;

rather, it inspires connections. The epistolary form embodies this desire. It seeks companionship, connecting speaker and addressee. Like a rhyme, one verse letter seems to demand another. To put this idea in reverse, each rhyme offers an epistle in miniature, awaiting a reply.

Crossing historical moments, the rhymes also restage intergenerational conflicts. Repeatedly the sequence refers to the legendary second Fisk University Black Writers' Conference held in 1967, invoking its contested legacy. In a highly compressed fashion, the poet refers to arguments that generations repeat like rituals. One passage describes a group poetry reading where "Kevin"—presumably Kevin Young, Jackson's fellow member of the Dark Room Collective— recalled how several speakers at the Fisk conference attacked Robert Hayden for allegedly shirking his responsibilities as a black poet and educator. As depicted in Jackson's poem, Young noted "[h]ow Fisk's unrewarded poet, an Auden/ Acolyte, went through the grinder/Of black scrutiny" (*H*, 119). Tellingly, the poem rhymes "Kevin" and "Hayden," suggesting how the repeated drama assigns each a similar role. As if seeking to reenact what a cultural historian has called the "process of scapegoating and ostracization" that Hayden suffered,[40] the older poets in attendance attacked Young and his contemporaries with "verbal blows that purged/Us from the thumb of the Black Arts" (*H*, 120). As presented in the poem, the older poets' hostility frees the next generation. Defiantly the rhyme royal form marks Jackson as another "Auden acolyte" released from "the thumb of the Black Arts." In the continued argument over the movement's legacy, the form aligns the younger poets with Hayden.

The verse form also signals a more respectful and complicated difference. The Fisk conference introduced

Gwendolyn Brooks to a new black aesthetic, inspiring a change in her poetry and social vision. Before the conference, Brooks observed, "I, too, had liked the sound of the word 'universal.' "[41] After it, she proclaimed that she shared the Black Arts Movement's interest in art "by blacks, about blacks, to blacks" (*CGB*, 120). In addition to her decision to switch from Harper & Row to black publishing houses, she also expressed her new commitments through her versification; in particular, she used forms more closely identified with a specific notion of African-American literary tradition. "No, I'm not writing sonnets, and I probably won't be," she explained, "because, as I've said many times, this does not seem to me to be a sonnet time."[42] Cagily Jackson regards this change, shifting metaphors. The poem mentions what it calls "[t]he conversion/In '67 at Fisk," asking, "Why dull the edge/Of a weapon?"(*H*, 71) Though Jackson ascribes these questions to "the critics," by implication it is clear he prefers Brooks's earlier aesthetic. Whereas Brooks characterizes her era as "not" "a sonnet time," Jackson presents "the times" as demanding a respect for ornate rhyme, which the rhyme royal form structures and respects. The technique seconds the claim: the "times" and "rhymes" belong with each other.

In addition the form recalls a specific genealogy. Though based on Auden's model, "Letter to Brooks" also evokes Brooks's earlier sequence, "The Anniad," which employed a variation of rhyme royal, and Sonia Sanchez's *Does Your House Have Lions?*,[43] a rhyme royal sequence inspired by Brooks's. "Letter to Brooks" does not return to the ideal Brooks scorned after Fisk; it does not seek to be "universal." Marked by a racial consciousness, Jackson pointedly asserts, "I write in the tradition" (*H*, 121), yet he defines "the tradition" differently than the Black Arts Movement did. It includes Brooks, Hayden, hip-hop artists, and Auden, a white Anglo-Nordic poet who addressed an English nobleman in a form that legend ascribes to James I and that Chaucer made famous. "Any half-decent rapper/Can conjure the dead," Thomas Sayers Ellis reports in "The Roll Call," concluding, "The trick is ancestral."[44] Revising this point, Jackson presents technique as "ancestral" and acquired; they offer a meeting ground for the dead and the living. As with the other writers under discussion, hip hop suggests excitement and potential: "Our brain matter's/ Amped, mic-checked." At the same time, it instills sensitivity, training the "brain" and "spirit." In this celebratory vision, hip hop's form, the movement of "mind" over "[b]eats and grooves," creates an idealized community.

As this gesture suggests, in "Erie" Jackson seeks to synthesize the techniques of print-based poetry and hip hop, using hip-hop rhyme in the rhyme royal stanza. Another kind of poem emulates hip hop even more directly; these works so closely imitate the formal properties, language, and style of the music that they resemble transcribed lyrics. As Kevin Coval boasts, they "mimic/the art/of the illest."[45] Other examples pay homage to particular performers, borrowing their artistic characteristics and personalities. "I'm that Black Elvis, that Black Bach," Terrance Hayes writes, ventriloquizing Kool Keith, incorporating his nicknames and peculiar sexual peccadilloes: "I'm too cool. I grind my pelvis, my back//crack, your mamma back crack too."[46] The opening poem of Hayes's influential earlier collection, *Hip Logic*, "emcee" strays from this close identification, exploring a more complicated relationship. Instead of assuming the performer's perspective the poem addresses him in the second person: "You get to wear triple X/Jeans for easy access to the lair of first breaths."[47] The speaker envies the emcee's outsized persona; his "triple X/Jeans," for instance, combines sartorial style and sexual opportunity, both apparently denied to the speaker. While the rhymes—"X," "access," and "breaths"—connect emcee and print-based poet, the perspective marks an essential difference, one that extends even into the realms of the imagination. "I had to get high to write this," the speaker admits.[48]

The most promising indication that contemporary poets have absorbed lessons from hip hop, though, remains poems where hip hop's influence remains less openly declared, where the lessons the music offers have been absorbed and its techniques recalibrated for the authors' own purposes. D. A. Powell's poems quote, parody, and rework a host of musical genres, including opera, gospel, and, most frequently, disco. Multiple poems, for instance, celebrate the androgynous singer Sylvester and the DJs of the disco era. "Heaven is a discotheque," one exclaims.[49] Hip hop appears less overtly, though attentive readers detect its hard-to-define traces. When an interviewer noted that Powell's poem "[dogs and boys can treat you like trash. and dogs do love trash]" has "a hip-hop feel," Powell clarified what the interviewer intuited. The poem, Powell noted, "has the triplet rhyming that you often find in rap. I must say that Sugarhill Gang and Grandmaster Flash were as important to me as Gertrude Stein and John Keats."[50]

Demonstrating this influence, a number of Powell's poems employ triplet rhyming. In "[this is what you love: more people: you remember]," for instance, the speaker addresses another gay man no longer involved in sexual pursuit:

> now you only regret men unbedded. unwedded to your cheek-y
> desire to lift strangers from taxis.   or texas: why be picky?

but now you've gone "gee" in your ratings: shirley temple and madeline

volunteer work.   neighborhood meetings.   you even bring the gelatine.[51]

To achieve the kinds of rhymes that hip-hop artists favor, Powell presents rhyming techniques more familiar to their art form than to print-based poetry. In print-based poetry, triplet rhyming most commonly takes the form of tercets, three-lined stanzas whose endwords rhyme. Robert Frost's "Provide, Provide," for instance, follows the definition Florio offered in the late sixteenth century: "a terset of rymes, rymes that ryme three and three":

> No memory of having starred
> Atones for later disregard
> Or keeps the end from being hard.[52]

Frost's triplet rhymes follow the organization of the poem's lines and stanzas; they establish a dependable meeting of clearly established formal obligations. In contrast, arranged in couplet stanzas, Powell's lines offer putatively "extra" rhymes: triplets and more. To do so, they perform a number of deft maneuvers. Like an emcee pausing to break a word in two, the hyphenated "cheek-y" elevates an unstressed syllable to a stress position. This gesture expands the word's sonic range, allowing it to rhyme a host of words that sound quite different, "taxis," "picky," "gee," and "shirley." Mixing off-rhyme and full, the poem encourages a similar pronunciation of "taxis" as if the word were stretched to three syllables. Presented in this fashion, "taxis" rhymes with two words that share no rhyming syllables: "picky" and "texas." Such techniques produce several interlocking rhyme schemes.

At least three such patterns coexist: the couplet stanzas; the triple rhyme of "cheek-y," "picky," and "taxis"; and the rhyming sets that rhyme with members of the triple rhyme set.

Just as the triple rhymes range beyond the stanza's borders, they also extend across the poem and even beyond it. Half the poem separates one of the triple rhyme's elements from the other: the "taxes [or texas?" that introduces the triplet in the fourth line and "taxis. Or texas" that concludes it in the twelfth. Even more dramatically, the poem ends with a triplet rhyme whose third member the poem never mentions. Preparation for this effect starts with the book's title. Introducing the collection's central metaphor, *Cocktails* refers both to alcoholic mixed drinks and to the medicines prescribed for HIV-positive patients (as well as the male anatomy). Like the two epigraphs it follows, the collection's opening poem reinforces the first two meanings, describing "the cocktail hour" in both senses (*C*, 3). "[this is what you love: more people: you remember]" appears as the collection's third poem. Alert to cocktail references, a reader hears the penultimate line, "you've gone 'gee' in your ratings: shirley temple and madeline," as referring both to the film star/gay icon Shirley Temple and to the nonalcoholic drink that bears her name. This suggestion offers a persuasive logic; the addressed man has turned childlike both in the movies he watches and in the drinks he consumes. The first word in the rhyme construction, "madeline," encourages this notion. Because "madeline" rhymes with so few words, it brings to mind "grenadine," the syrup that serves as one of a Shirley Temple's main ingredients. Withholding the expected word, the poem ends with a jarring, unidiomatic rhyme, "you even bring the gelatine." In this context, "gelatine" offers a pretentious malapropism, a mispronunciation of "gelatin," that is, "Jell-O," the archetypal déclassé food served at "neighborhood meetings." The effectively forced rhyme achieves several effects. It suggests the falseness of the identity that the addressed man has assumed, the new lifestyle that fits him as awkwardly as the rhyme. The ghost rhyme, the tercet's third rhyme word, contrasts the speaker's less restrained ways with his friend's; in essence, the addressed man's life has turned into one endless Shirley Temple cocktail. Pulling off a harder trick, the rhyme makes the insult sound flirtatious, tempting the addressed man to reverse his ways and enjoy certain adult pleasures.

This rhyming style echoes the poem's subject. Seemingly incompatible words rhyme and form improbable combinations, as if undoing the lost opportunities that the poem describes: "now you only regret men unbedded." Promiscuous, the rhymes enact a coupling in place of this remorse. As elsewhere in Powell's work, they remain archly sexy even when depicting grim or sad subject matter. Introducing his earlier collection, *Tea*, Powell recalled how, when writing those poems, he was "reenacting the serial polygamy that had characterized my life.... I had moved through the world a sexual libertine, unfaithful even in the way I conflated the touch of one lover with thoughts of another" (*T*, xi). Powell's rhyming style might be characterized similarly as "serial polygamy."

To compare Powell's poetry with its formal influences is to see how much it transforms them. In the late 1970s and early 1980s, the Sugar Hill Gang and Grandmaster Flash established hip hop's commercial potential with two hits: respectively, "Rapper's Delight," a party record set to the bassline of "Good Times," and "The Message," a landmark in "message" or "political" hip hop. Employing the triplet rhyme Powell would borrow, "The Message" cautions its listeners to avoid the mistakes that doomed the song's protagonist, an imprisoned dropout. "Turned stick-up kid, but look what you done did," the song knowingly recalls, describing the teen's final humiliation, one that drove him to commit suicide:

> Got sent up for a eight-year bid
> Now your manhood is took and you're a Maytag
> Spend the next two years as a undercover fag.[53]

"Rapper's Delight" maintains a more lighthearted tone. Switching insults from "fag" to "fairy," the Sugar Hill Gang's Big Bank Hank offers a cartoonish homophobic jibe, not a nightmare vision of repeated homosexual rape. To convince a woman identified as "Lois Lane" to leave her boyfriend, Big Bank Hank decries his sexual rival, Superman: "He's a fairy, I do suppose/ Flyin' through the air in pantyhose."[54] To recast the same form, Powell, a poet of gay male sexual congress in virtually all its forms, details pleasures quite at odds with those that hip hop typically admits. His poetry does not reverse hip hop's sexual politics so much as set it aside and redefine the form for its own purposes. In lines such as "the boys are fickle when they lick you. they stick you with twigs/and roll you over like roaches" (*C*, 14), Powell suggests how flexible this kind of rhyming can be, how many of its possibilities remain unexplored.

To find rhyme's greatest resources, Powell draws a model from music, not print-based poetry. Rhyme, Harryette Mullen insisted, "is too powerful a tool to be abandoned to advertising, greeting cards, or even platinum rap recordings." Contemporary poets face a historical reversal; in Mullen's terms, they must "reclaim" a technique once intimately associated with their art.[55] The current generation of younger poets came of age when, with few exceptions, the major American poets did not rhyme, and those who did typically used the technique to signal more a remove from contemporary life than an openness to it. In contrast hip-hop artists centered their songs on this technique. They bragged about their "rhymes of strength and powers."[56] Hip-hop songs rhyme consistently, cunningly, and with a flair that challenges listeners not attuned to their daring. "In rap," the poet James Fenton insists, "a very low standard is set for rhyme."[57] It is more accurate to say that the standard that print-based poetry sets for rhyme remains low: tame, tentative, and unappealing. Each new generation of artists reevaluates the previous, redefining what is compelling and overrated. Poems such as Powell's turn to hip-hop rhyming as a source of vitality; they synthesize its lessons with those acquired from their own art form. They start the process of reevaluation and reclamation.

CONCLUSION

On the Present and Future of Rhyme

FIRST PUBLISHED IN 1897, RUDYARD Kipling's "White Horses" ends:

> To mill your foeman's armies—
> To bray his camps abroad—
> Trust ye the wild white horses
> The Horses of the Lord![1]

When in 1903 Kipling collected the poem in *The Five Nations*, he changed the passage's first two lines, "To bray your foeman's armies—/To chill and snap his sword—."[2] The revision neatened a partial rhyme of "abroad"/"Lord," converting it into the full rhyme "sword"/"Lord." Despite Kipling's housekeeping efforts, his verse did not escape censure. In his monograph *A Study of Versification,* Brander Matthews cited the first version's rhyme of "abroad"/"Lord" as one example of "atrocious rhymes" produced by "great" "poets." "[I]t is a fact," Matthews lamented, "that many poets of high distinction have on occasion fallen from grace and descended to marry pairs of words which protested more or less violently against the wedding."[3] In a letter to Matthews, Kipling objected to the example but accepted the principle: "Maybe I've rhymed 'abroad' with Lord more than once but I think, the only time I did it consciously I corrected in another edition" (*LRK*, 34).

Only a few decades later, there remained no need to object. Such rhymes achieved a new status as perfectly "correct." In a 1933 verse epistle, "A Letter to My Aunt Discussing the Correct Approach to Modern Poetry," Dylan Thomas self-deprecatingly uses this term in order to report, "Do not forget that 'limpet' rhymes/With 'strumpet' in these troubled times."[4] Poking fun at his own fashionable practice, his own "correct approach," the author of the verse epistle reminds readers what they already know. The words do not "protest" their pairing as a violation of decorum. Instead, as T. V. F. Brogan notes, "[S]uch practice is to be seen not as a falling away from a standard but as a redefinition of that standard."[5] In the intervening years, literary fashion redefined the very nature of sounds understood to "rhyme."

As this example suggests and historical studies confirm,[6] rhyming decorum changes across eras and cultures. Rhymes once deemed proper are redefined as déclassé; rhymes once decried as clumsy ¹are celebrated as daring. Already in its short history, hip hop has undergone several revolutions in rhyme, moving from often monosyllabic end-stopped rhyme to denser patterns of internal and end rhymes. At each stage, the art has veered farther from the most prestigious forms of print-based poetry. Hip hop emphasizes the most audacious, seemingly incongruous rhymes, the cobbling together of heterogeneous sonic and semantic material. Conspicuously hip-hop performers increasingly favor the particular kinds of rhymes that the most prestigious forms of modern and contemporary poetry generally avoid, associating them with unskilled or comic verse. A single quatrain by Eminem features more examples of identical, multisyllabic, forced, and mosaic rhyme than an entire volume of *The Best American Poetry* anthology. Remembering his artistic training, Jay-Z describes how he also relished similarly ornate techniques; he "loved rhyming for the sake of rhyming, purely for the aesthetics of the rhyme itself—the challenge of moving around couplets and triplets, stacking double entendres."[7]

"[T]o entertain and to dazzle with creative rhymes,"[8] such artists conspicuously employ techniques that the hip-hop predecessors they venerate also avoided. Techniques such as triple rhyme and internal rhyme entered the music in the mid- to late 1980s and then developed into the new standard. "The first rap song I ever heard was Ice-T, 'Reckless,'" recalls Eminem. "I was fascinated." Along with other songs of the period, "Reckless" inspired the nine-year-old future performer: "I wanted to do it, to rhyme."[9] "Reckless" features end-stopped rhyming couplets. Fastidiously the syntax and lineation align and the song avoids multisyllabic rhymes. With a few exceptions, one- and two-syllable words dominate the song's vocabulary. When the song introduces multisyllabic end words, it rhymes with only one of the available syllables. Even as the performers assert their music's singularity, "This high-powered music is truly unique./As The Glove cuts the rhythm to the hip-hop beat,"[10] the song carefully follows the historical moment's rather limited rhyming conventions. The next generation crafted rhymes from the possibilities that "Reckless" left unexplored. They centered songs on the hints they found in the work of innovators such as Eric B, Rakim, and Big Daddy Kane; they repositioned novelties as central to the art. "I rap for listeners, bluntheads, fly ladies, and prisoners," Nas famously boasts a decade later, rhyming "listeners" both internally, with "prisoners," and with the word that ends the following line, "niggas."[11] He opens the song with a multisyllabic rhyme that combines internal and end rhyme. Inspired by such models, the art voraciously assimilated new techniques. Fashioned on the cusp of this change, "Reckless" proclaims its formal greatness, but the subsequent decades produced the more energetic rhymes.

As it matured, hip hop benefited from certain linguistic resources. During the last few decades, the English language has undergone an amazing expansion. According to one scholarly study, 8,500 new words enter the language each year. Over fifty years, the size of the language grew by more than 70 percent: from 597,000 words in 1950 to 1,022,000 in 2000.[12] Technology both generates neologisms and extends previously existing words into new contexts and grammatical functions.[13] Noting that the 1980s and 1990s featured a great increase in new words, the authors of another recent study credit "new digital media" "which offer new environments for the evolutionary dynamics of word use."[14] While the particular numbers involved may be debated, the research supports the widely held perception that English surges forward with incredible velocity. New technologies both publicize new words and hasten their wider use, encouraging what the authors call "a dramatic increase in the relative use ('utility') of newborn words over the last 20–30 years" ("SLGF," 3). As these studies suggest, English claims many more words than previously and those new words achieve popularity more quickly. In blunt terms, the contemporary moment excels at creating new words in English and rapidly spreading them.

Of all the verbal arts, hip hop remains the most alert to these conditions; they serve as the linguistic environment in which the music arose and flourished. As the studies suggest, the dates of English's most dramatic expansion roughly parallel those of the music's. This historical good fortune boosted hip hop; it offered its artists significant rhyming opportunities. It made the new style of virtuoso rhyming possible. "Look at what I'm dropping here," Lupe Fiasco commands. "Do this for the block and the blogosphere."[15] As these lines assert, the art couples the local and international, a single syllable and a multisyllabic word, the "real" and "virtual." The alliterative phrase connects words whose history nearly equals America's. According to the *Oxford English Dictionary*, "block" first appears in English in 1796 and "blogosphere" in 1999. The couplet rhyme bridges a much longer period: "here" first appears in English in 825, more than a thousand years before "blogosphere." The newest word might be the most prominent, but the lines artfully mix the new and old. With deceptively casual ease, they celebrate the language's history and its present.

"Every reformation in English poetry," Anne Ferry notes, "has involved shifts in attitudes toward rhyming, in the practices of it, and in the rules for its proper conduct."[16] If, to borrow a phrase from Sir Philip Sidney, the English Renaissance's "mingled language" found its greatest artistic expression in the sonnet,[17] the contemporary moment's linguistic expansion also offers new "attitudes," rules, and strategies for rhyming. Recounting his own experiences, Robyn Creswell, the current poetry editor of the *Paris Review* and a translator of French and Arabic literature, suggests a broader development:

> Most of the poems stuck in my head are rap songs. Rap is the music I grew up listening to, and the lyrics from those days,

the late eighties and early nineties, have stayed with me. I've forgotten most of the poems I had to memorize at school; of Keats's "To Autumn," I remember only the famous lines. On the other hand, Big Daddy Kane's "Smooth Operator," Rakim's "Mahogany," or Nas's "N.Y. State of Mind"—these are poems I know by heart, from beginning to end, and will probably never forget.[18]

As all those songs stuck in our heads confirm, the nature of rhyme has changed. It has grown more confident and assertive; it claims the airwaves and Internet; it swaggers and seduces. Attentive to the sounds that surround them, hip-hop artists remain the most interesting contemporary rhymers. Instead of isolating themselves from a potential source of vitality, they listen hard, hearing—and expanding—the range of available resources. We live in era of virtuoso rhyming, awaiting only the print-based poets' full contribution.

CREDITS

Earlier versions of some of this chapters appeared in *Virginia Quarterly Review* (spring 2012), *The Princeton Encyclopedia of Poetry and Poetics*, Fourth Edition, *The Poetics of Song Lyrics, A Companion to Poetic Genre*, and *The Antioch Review* (winter 2009).

Pink Cookies In A Plastic Bag Getting Crushed By Buildings
Words and Music by David Porter, James Todd Smith and Marlon
Williams Copyright (c) 1993 IRVING MUSIC, INC., UNIVERSAL
MUSIC CORP., LL COOL J MUSIC and MARLEY MARL MUSIC,
INC. All Rights for MARLEY MARL MUSIC Controlled and
Administered by EMI APRIL MUSIC INC (ASCAP) All Rights
Reserved International Copyright Secured Used by Permission
Reprinted with Permission of Hal Leonard Corporation.

Boring Words and Music by Allison Pierce, Catherine Pierce and
Roger Greenawalt
  Copyright (c) 2007 MULTISONGS, BUNNY CAT MUSIC,
FAMOUS MUSIC LLC., and WOMAN IN Y MUSIC All Rights
for BUNNY CAT MUSIC Controlled and Administered by
MULTISONGS All Rights Reserved Used by Permission *Reprinted
with Permission of Hal Leonard Corporation.*

Mirror Words and Music by Shaffer Smith and Robert Shea Taylor
Copyright (c) 2006 by Zomba Songs, Super Sayin Publishing, 1996
Music Lane Publishing and N. 22nd Publishing
  All Rights for Super Sayin Publishing Administered by Zomba
Songs All Rights for 1996 Music Lane Publishing and N. 22nd
Publishing Administered by Cherry Lane Music Publishing
Company, Inc. International Copyright Secured All Rights
Reserved *Reprinted with Permission of Hal Leonard Corporation.*

Gold Digger Words and Music by Kanye West, Ray Charles and
Renald Richard
  (c) 2005 EMI BLACKWOOD MUSIC INC., PLEASE GIMME
MY PUBLISHING and UNICHAPPELL MUSIC INC. All Rights for
PLEASE GIMME MY PUBLISHING Controlled and Administered
by EMI BLACKWOOD MUSIC INC. All Rights Reserved
International Copyright Secured Used by Permissioncontains a
sample of "I've Got A Woman" by Ray Charles and Renald Richard
(c) 1954 (Renewed) Unichappell Music, Inc.
  Reprinted with Permission of Hal Leonard Corporation.

NOTES

Introduction

1. Donald Davie, *Collected Poems* (Chicago: University of Chicago Press, 1991), 166.
2. Paul Collins, "The Lost Symphony," *Believer*, November 2004, 11.
3. Nas, "Hip Hop Is Dead," *Hip Hop Is Dead* (Def Jam, 2006).
4. Harryette Mullen, *Sleeping with the Dictionary* (Berkeley: University of California Press, 2002), 42.
5. The band reportedly credited its name to Art Janov's Primal Scream, though I have been unable to find the specific phrase there.
6. George Strait, "All My Ex's [*sic*] Live in Texas," *Ocean Front Property* (MCA Records, 1987).
7. Drake, "HYFR," *Take Care* (Cash Money Record, 2011).
8. See http://pentametron.com/.
9. For the most recent jeremiad on this subject, see Mark Edmundson's "Poetry Slam: Or, The Decline of American Verse," *Harper's*, July 18, 2013.
10. Studies of rhyme in rock, for instance, tend to focus on single artists who show exceptional interest in and talent with the technique. For a particularly thoughtful and

influential recent example, see Christopher Ricks's *Dylan's Vision of Sin* (New York: Ecco, 2003), 30–48. For a treatment of popular poetry in the first half of the twentieth century, see Mike Chasar, *Everyday Reading: Poetry and Popular Culture in Modern America* (New York: Columbia University Press, 2012).

11. Though hip hop enjoys a global reach, I focus on the American context, which serves as both the music's national epicenter and the sharpest point of contrast with the most prestigious forms of print-based poetry. As comparativist approaches reveal, different national and cultural contexts reconfigure the connections that I will explore. Limiting my study to American hip-hop artists, poets, and critics and to international figures whose work exerts considerable influence on the contemporary American musical and literary scene also necessarily helps to manage an otherwise impossibly broad topic. For a sense of hip hop's immense international reach and the scholarship on it, see Alain-Philippe Durand, *Black, Blanc, Beur: Rap Music and Hip-Hop Culture in the Francophone World* (Lanham, MD: Scarecrow, 2002), Ian Maxwell, *Phat Beats, Dope Rhymes: Hip Hop Down Under Comin' Upper* (Middletown, CT: Wesleyan University Press, 2001), and Tony Mitchell, *Global Noise: Rap and Hip Hop Outside the USA* (Middletown, CT: Wesleyan University Press, 2001). It is also important to note that other nations and cultures retain more entrenched traditions of print-based rhyming poetry. The Irish poet Michael Longley, for instance, a little testily observes, "A lot of modern poetry, I insist, does rhyme," citing the work of his countrymen Seamus Heaney, Derek Mahon, and Paul Muldoon. "I regret not using rhyme more frequently," however, he also notes. See Tony Curtis, *How Poets Work* (Brigend, Wales: Seren, 1996), 118.

12. A notable exception remains the group of largely American poets known as the "new formalists," who, emerging in the late 1980s, promoted the use of metrical verse technique and rhyme. Tellingly, though, the majority of the poems written by poets associated with this group do not rhyme.

For a witty manifesto in defense of rhyme written by a poet often associated with the group, see A. E. Stallings's "Presto Manifesto!" *Poetry Magazine,* February 2009, available online at http://www.poetryfoundation.org/poetrymagazine/article/182841.

In a blog post, "Rhyme Driven," the writer somewhat wearily concedes, "Of course, let's admit it: rhyme is something of a special case in English." See "Rhyme Driven," Harriet, Poetry Foundation, January 2008, available at http://www.poetryfoundation.org/harriet/2008/01/rhyme-driven/.

For an overview of the new formalism, see David Caplan, "What Was New Formalism?" *A Companion to Poetic Genre,* ed. Erik Martiny (Oxford: Wiley-Blackwell, 2011), 17–33.

13. Natsuko Tsujimura and Stuart Davis, "Dragon Ash and the Reinterpretation of Hip Hop: On the Notion of Rhyme in Japanese Hip Hop," *Global Linguistic Flows: Hip Hop Cultures, Youth Identities, and the Politics of Language*, ed. H. Samy Alim, Awad Ibrahim, and Alastair Pennycook (New York: Taylor and Francis, 2009), 182. See also Ian Condry, *Hip-Hop Japan: Rap and the Paths of Cultural Globalization* (Durham, NC: Duke University Press, 2006).

14. Andrew Osborn, "Skirmishes on the Border: The Evolution and Function of Paul Muldoon's Fuzzy Rhyme," *Contemporary Literature* 41, no. 2 (2000): 323.

15. In addition to the other examples discussed here, see also Nicholson Baker, *The Anthologist* (New York: Simon and Schuster, 2009), whose main character obsesses at great length over "the death of rhyme" and debates who rightly bears the "blame" (130) for this situation, and John Irving, *The Hotel New Hampshire* (New York: Random House, 1981), where a bearded intellectual coffeehouse intellectual pontificates on "the death of rhyme": "And when he moved onto the novel, I thought I had better pay up and leave. My waiter was busy so I had to listen to the death of plot and characterization. Among the many deaths the man described, he included the death of sympathy" (294).

16. Tobias Wolff, *Old School* (New York: Random House, 2003), 44; hereafter cited in the text as *OS*.

17. A scene that takes place a few pages later suggests the genealogy of the student's ideas.

One of his teachers asks Frost a question after the poet's reading. After the teacher mistakenly refers to Frost's famous poem as "Stopping in Woods," he opines that "such a rigidly formal arrangement is inadequate to express the modern consciousness" (*OS*, 51–52). Icily Frost icily asks what "modern consciousness" means and the teacher recites a trite litany straight from the classroom, listing "the mind's response to industrialization, the saturation propaganda of governments and advertisers, two world wars, the concentration camps, the dimming of faith by science, and of course the constant threat of nuclear annihilation" (*OS*, 52). In the teacher's unwelcomed minilecture, the reader hears the origin of the student's complaint. Exchanging vulgarity for bombast, the student borrows his teacher's clichés.

18. Matthew Zapruder, "Off The Shelf: Finding the Pieces that Turn Writing into Poetry," *Los Angeles Times*, September 20, 2009, available at http://www.latimes.com/entertainment/news/arts/la-caw-off-the-shelf20-2009sep20,0,4631326.

19. T. S. Eliot, *The Complete Poems and Plays, 1909–1950* (New York: Harcourt, Brace, and World, 1971).

20. John Berryman, *The Freedom of the Poet* (New York: Farrar, Straus and Giroux, 1976), 270; hereafter cited in the text as *FP*.

21. "[A]n expectation has been created," observes Berryman, "only to be diminished or destroyed" (*FP*, 270).

22. Daniel Albright, "Modernist Poetic Form," *The Cambridge Companion to Twentieth-Century English Poetry*, ed. Neil Corcoran (Cambridge: Cambridge University Press, 2007), 26.

23. Glyn Maxwell, *Atlantic Unbound*, June 2001, available athttp://www.theatlantic.com/past/docs/unbound/poetry/maxwell.htm .

24. Jay-Z, "The Audacity of Hope," *Vibe*, September 2008, 128.

25. 50 Cent, "Patiently Waiting," *Get Rich or Die Tryin'* (Aftermath Entertainment, 2003); Rick Ross, *God Forgives, I Don't* (Def Jam, 2012); Kanye West, "Apologize," *Freshmen Adjustment* (mixtape, 2005); Country Grammar, *Never Let 'Em C U Sweat*

(Fo' Reel Records, 2000); and Lupe Fiasco, "Diddy" (freestyle), *Super Stardom Mixtape* (mixtape, 2011).

26. Eminem, "Must Be the Ganja," *Relapse* (Interscope, 2009) and "Just Don't Give a Fuck," *The Slim Shady LP* (Aftermath, 1999).

27. Kanye West, "Jesus Walks," *The College Dropout* (Roc-A-Fella, 2004).

28. Wallace Stevens, *Letters of Wallace Stevens*, ed. Holly Stevens (Berkeley: University of California Press, 1996), 157.

29. Alexander Pope," "An Essay on Criticism," *Classic Writings on Poetry*, ed. William Harmon (New York: Columbia University Press, 2003), 218; hereafter cited in the text as *CW*.

30. Eminem featuring Eye-Kyu, "Searchin'," *Infinite* (Web Entertainment, 1996).

31. West, "Jesus Walks."

32. Kanye West, "All Falls Down," *The College Dropout* (Roc-A-Fella, 2004).

33. The Dead Prez, "Hip Hop," *Let's Get Free* (Loud Records, 2000).

34. Big Daddy Kane and DJ Mister Cee, "DJs Get No Credit," *Prince of Darkness* (Cold Chillin' Records, 1991).

35. S. Craig Watkins, *Hip Hop Matters* (Boston: Beacon, 2005), 13. As I will discuss shortly, the literature detailing hip hop's social and cultural history and development is deep and rich. In addition to the other texts quoted here and subsequently, of particular help to me have been Jeff Change, *Can't Stop Won't Stop: A History of the Hip-Hop Generation* (New York: Picador, 2005); the essays included in Murray Forman and Mark Anthony Neal, eds., *That's the Joint! The Hip-Hop Studies Reader* (New York: Routledge, 2004); and Marcus Reeves, *Somebody Scream! Rap Music's Rise to Prominence in the Aftershock of Black Power* (New York: Faber and Faber, 2008). See also Tricia Rose's landmark study, *Black Noise: Rap Music and Black Culture in Contemporary America* (Middletown, CT: Wesleyan University Press, 1994).

36. Paul Edwards, *How to Rap: The Art and Science of the Hip-Hop MC* (Chicago: Chicago Review Press, 2009), 83.

37. See Susan B. A. Somers-Willett, *The Cultural Politics of Slam Poetry: Race, Identity, and the Performance of Popular Verse in America* (Ann Arbor: University of Michigan Press,

2009), 19. I also draw from its description of slam poetry's development (3–4).

38. *Burning Down the House: Selected Poems from the Nuyorican Poets' Cafe's National Slam Champions*, ed. R. Bonair-Agard et al. (New York: Soft Skull, 2000), 69, 71.

39. Richard Shusterman, *Performing Live: Aesthetic Alternatives for the Ends of Life* (Ithaca, NY: Cornell University Press, 2000), 37.

40. See Imani Perry, *Prophets of the Hood: Politics and Poetics in Hip Hop* (Durham, NC: Duke University Press, 2004).

41. Ta-Nehisi Coates, "Keepin' It Unreal: $elling the Myth of Bla¢k Male Violen¢e, Long Past Its Expiration Date," *Da Capo Best Music Writing 2004: The Year's Finest Writing on Rock, Hip-Hop, Jazz, Pop, Country, and More*, ed. Mickey Hart (New York: Da Capo, 2005), 51–59.

42. See, for instance, Rose, *Black Noise*, 3: "Rap's stories continue to articulate the shifting terms of black marginality in contemporary American culture."

43. Adam Bradley, *Book of Rhymes: The Poetics of Hip Hop* (New York: Basic Books, 2009), xii. Distinguishing between what he calls rap's "new-school music" and "old-school poetry" (xv), to a certain extent, Bradley anticipates certain of my objections. As we shall see, though, my argument departs from his in several ways. Most significantly, as I will argue, hip hop's commitment to rhyme signals a commitment to the contemporary moment. In this respect, paradoxically the most prestigious forms of contemporary poetry might offer the more old-fashioned poetics or, in Bradley's terms, the "old-school poetry."

44. Adam Bradley and Andrew DuBois, eds., *The Anthology of Rap* (New Haven, CT: Yale University Press, 2010), xxix.

45. Quoted in Victor D. Infante, "Stranded: Poet Mark Strand Preaches Political Indifference at UCI," *Orange County Weekly*, February 10, 2000, available at http://www.ocweekly. com/2000-02-10/culture/stranded.

46. In a review, the poetry scholar David Bromwich lays bare this assumption. He hardens the distinction between the two art forms, asserting, "If poetry attempts to widen imagination,

rap aims to narrow it." Attacked by a reader for "his ignorance about his subject," Bromwich replies:

> I do not claim to be an authority on rap. I have heard about as much of it as the average father of two American boys can expect to have heard by the time the boys are in their teens. But that is more than my questioner may be aware of. As music, it lacks music; as poetry, it lacks art.

David Bromwich, "David Bromwich Replies," *New Republic*, December 2 and 9, 2002, 4.

A lack of knowledge, let alone expertise, does not stop Strand and Bromwich from discussing hip hop because they see the subject as both transparently obvious and loathsome: it requires only a passing familiarity to judge its achievement as "music," "poetry," and "art." They present their ignorance as a virtue, a rejection of an imagination-killing menace. In essence they boast of their inattention.

47. T. S. Eliot, *Selected Prose of T. S. Eliot*, ed. Frank Kermode (New York: Farrar, Straus and Giroux, 1975), 43.

48. Charles Bernstein, *My Way: Speeches and Poems* (Chicago: University of Chicago Press, 1999), 11.

49. Thom Gunn, *The Man with Night Sweats* (New York: Farrar, Straus and Giroux, 1992), 45.

50. William Wordsworth, *Selected Poems*, ed. John O. Hayden (New York: Penguin, 1994), 65. I would like to thank my colleague Mark Allison for bringing this second reference to my attention.

51. Jorge Luis Borges, "The Divine Comedy," *The Poets' Dante: Twentieth-Century Responses*, ed. Peter Hawkins and Rachel Jacoff (New York: Farrar, Straus and Giroux, 2001), 121.

52. Jay Z, "Renegade," *The Blueprint* (Roc-A-Fella, 2001).

53. Jay-Z, *Decoded* (New York: Spiegel and Grau, 2010), 308.

54. H. Samy Alim, "Interview with Mos Def," *Tha Global Cipha: Hip Hop Culture and Consciousness*, ed. James G. Spady, H. Samy Alim, and Samir Meghelli (Philadelphia: Black History Museum Publishers, 2006), 126.

55. John Bayley, *Selected Essays* (Cambridge: Cambridge University Press, 1984), 149.

56. Leslie A. Fiedler, *No! In Thunder: Essays on Myth and Literature* (New York: Stein and Day, 1972), 25. T. S. Eliot's description of how a similar understanding of the relative openness of Italian and English to rhyme affected his composition of "Little Gidding":

> My first problem was to find an approximation to *terza rima* without rhyming. English is less copiously provided with rhyming words than Italian; and those rhymes we have are in a way more emphatic. The rhyming words call too much attention to themselves: Italian is the one language known to me in which exact rhyme can always achieve its effect—and what the effect of rhyme is, for the neurologist rather than the poet to investigate—without the risk of obtruding itself. I therefore adopted, for my purpose, a simple alternation of unrhymed masculine and feminine terminations, as the nearest way of giving the light effect of rhyme in Italian.

> See T. S. Eliot, *To Criticize the Critic and Other Writings* (New York: Farrar, Straus and Giroux, 1965), 128.

57. Quoted in Mona Van Duyn, untitled essay, *Ecstatic Occasions, Expedient Forms*, ed. David Lehman (Ann Arbor: University of Michigan Press, 1999), 215.

58. Frank Kermode, *Shakespeare, Spenser, Donne* (Abington, UK: Routledge, 2005), 270.

59. " 'Hussein' Chant at Palin Rally," *The Caucus: The Government and Politics Blog of the Times*, November 1, 2008, available at http://thecaucus.blogs.nytimes.com/2008/11/01/hussein-chant-at-palin-rally/.

60. To the best of my knowledge, the artist has not been identified. See http://politicalhumor.about.com/od/sarahpalin/ig/Sarah-Palin-Pictures/Nope.-XYh.htm.

61. *The Advocate*, September 2009, cover.

62. D. A. Powell, *Tea* (Middletown, CT: Wesleyan University Press, 1988), 46; hereafter cited in the text as *T*.

63. Tyrone Hayes, Kelly Haston, Mable Tsui, Anhthu Hoang, Cathryn Haeffele, and Aaron Vonk, "Atrazine-Induced Hermaphroditism at 0.1 ppb in American Leopard Frogs (*Rana pipiens*): Laboratory and Field Evidence," available at

http://www.ncbi.nlm.nih.gov/pmc/articles/PMC1241446/
pdf/ehp0111-000568.pdf.

64. Tryone Hayes, "The Atrazine Rap," http://www.youtube.com/
watch?v=3MxrH4lN0-A, uploaded March 2008.

65. Dashka Slater, "The Frog of War," *Mother Jones*, January/
February 2012, 44–67, available at http://www.motherjones.
com/environment/2011/11/tyrone-hayes-atrazine-syngenta-f
eud-frog-endangered?page=1. See also Elana Schor, "Enviro
Groups Cheer as Scientist Bombards Agribusiness with
Profane E-Mails," *New York Times*, August 26, 2010, available at http://www.nytimes.com/gwire/2010/08/26/26greenw
ire-enviro-groups-cheer-as-scientist-bombards-agri-18199.
html?pagewanted=all; and Elizabeth Royte, "Transsexual
Frogs," *Discover Magazine*, posted online February 1, 2003,
available at http://discovermagazine.com/2003/feb/featfrogs/.

In addition to the other articles and primary documents
previously noted, my summary of these events draws from
Slater's investigative account.

66. Alan Nadel, Litigation Counsel, Syngenta Crop Protection,
Inc., letter to Russel Gould, Chair, The Regents of the
University of California, et al., dated July 19, 2010.

67. Tyrone Hayes, email dated September 14, 2009, recipient's
name redacted.

68. Tyrone Hayes, email dated December 20, 2005, recipient's
name redacted.

69. LL Cool J, "Rock the Bells," *Radio* (Def Jam, 1985).

70. Tyrone Hayes, email dated February 13, 2009, recipient's name
redacted.

71. Tyrone Hayes, email dated February 23, 2010, recipient's name
redacted.

72. Alex Avery, "The Strange Case of Dr. Tyrone Hayes," *Atrazine
News*, July 29, 2010, available at http://atrazine.blogspot.com/
search/?q=tyrone+hayes.

73. "Self-Proclaimed Anti-Atrazine Activist Researcher Damages
His Already Shaky Cred with E-Mails," *Kansas Grains*,
July 29, 2010, available at http://kansasgrains.wordpress.
com/2010/07/29/self-proclaimed-anti-atrazine-activist-
researcher-damages-his-already-shaky-cred-with-e-mails/.

74. See *City of Greenville v. Syngenta Crop Protection, Inc., and Syngenta AG*, Case No. 3:10-cv-00188-JPG-PMF, available at http://www.atrazinesettlement.com/.

75. Paul de Man, *Resistance to Theory* (Minneapolis: University of Minnesota Press, 1986), 66.

Chapter 1

1. I take the details of the case from the court opinion, *Porreco v. Porreco*, 811 A.2d 566 (Pa. 2002); hereafter cited in the text as *PP*.

2. Hugh Kenner, *Historical Fictions: Essays* (Athens: University of Georgia Press, 1995), 283.

3. Hillary Rodham Clinton, *It Takes a Village: And Other Lessons Children Teach Us* (New York: Simon and Schuster, 2006), 137. Clinton recalls the title poem of Wallace Tipp's *A Great Big Ugly Man Came Up and Tied His Horse to Me: A Book of Nonsense Verse* (New York: Little, Brown, 1973).

4. John Milton, *Complete Poems and Major Prose* (Indianapolis, IN: Hackett, 2003), 210; and Philip Sidney, *Sidney's "The Defence of Poesy" and Selected Renaissance Literary Criticism*, ed. Gavin Alexander (New York: Penguin, 2004), 52.

5. Jonathan Swift, *The Works of the Rev. Jonathan Swift, D.D....: With Notes, Historical and Critical,* vol. 8, ed. John Nichols (New York: William Durell, 1812), 68.

6. Hugh A. C. Swinburne, review in *Fortnightly Review*, October 1867, rpt. in *Matthew Arnold: Prose Writings, Volume 2: The Poetry*, ed. Carl Dawson and John Pfordresher (London: Routledge, 1995), 182. Writing about the nineteenth century, Peter McDonald similarly notes, "[R]hyme was a shared idiom, without which the lyric was all but unthinkable." See *Sound Intentions: The Workings of Rhyme in Nineteenth-Century Poetry* (Oxford: Oxford University Press, 2012), 7.

7. Matthew Arnold, *On Translating Homer* (London: Smith, Elder, 1896), 15.

8. Jorge Luis Borges, *Borges on Writing*, ed. Norman Thomas di Giovanni, Daniel Halpern, and Frank MacShane (New York: Ecco, 1973), 141.

9. Robert Hass, *Now and Then: The Poet's Choice Columns, 1997–2000* (New York: Counterpoint, 2007), 256. In *The Art of Translating Poetry*, Burton Raffel similarly comments on one of his translations that "[i]n an attempt to convey all the poetry the original has to offer, this version does not rhyme." The implication is fairly clear: rhyme is not classified as part of "all the poetry." See *The Art of Translating Poetry* (University Park: Pennsylvania University Press, 1988), 20.

10. J. Paul Hunter, "Sleeping Beauties: Are Historical Aesthetics Worth Recovering?" *Eighteenth-Century Studies* 34, no. 1 (2000): 2; hereafter cited as "SB."

11. Marjorie Perloff and Robert von Hallberg, "Dialogue on Evaluation in Poetry," *Professions: Conversations on the Future of Literary and Cultural Studies*, ed. Donald Hall (Urbana: University of Illinois Press, 2001), 95.

12. Marjorie Perloff, *Rhyme and Meaning in the Poetry of Yeats*, De Proprietatibus litterarum, series practica, no. 5 (The Hague: Mouton & Co., 1970).

13. Lyn Hejinian, *The Language of Inquiry* (Berkeley: University of California Press, 2000), 307.

14. Ezra Pound, *Literary Essays*, ed. Thomas Stearns Eliot (London: Faber and Faber, 1954), 7.

15. *Merriam-Webster's Rhyming Dictionary: A Guide to Creating Lyrical Expressions* (New York: Merriam-Webster, 2001), 263.

16. *Browning-Ferris Industries of Vermont, Inc. v. Kelco Disposal, Inc.*, 492 US 257 (1989) 290; hereafter cited in the text as *BF*.

17. Jay Parini, "Introduction," *The Columbia History of American Poetry: Lustra to Mauberley*, ed. Jay Parini and Brett Candlish Millier (New York: Columbia University Press, 1993), xxv.

18. *The American Heritage Dictionary of the English Language*, 4th ed. (Boston: Houghton Mifflin, 2000).

19. See George Saintsbury, "Appendix III: The Nature and Phenomena of Doggerel," *A History of English Prosody from the Twelfth Century to the Present Day*, vol. 1, *From the Origins to Spenser* (New York: Macmillan, 1906), 413–416, 392; hereafter cited in the text as *HEP*. For a sensitive consideration of the challenges that contemporary doggerel faces, see David Rothman, "Ars Doggerel," *Expansive Poetry & Music Online,* available at http://expansivepoetryonline.com/journal/cult0297.html.

20. Northrop Frye, *The Well-Tempered Critic* (Bloomington: Indiana University Press, 1963), 69; hereafter cited in the text as *WTC*.

21. Northrop Frye, *Fables of Identity: Studies in Poetic Mythology* (New York: Harcourt, Brace, and World, 1963), 183.

22. Eakin admitted as much when he told a reporter, "I would never do it in a serious criminal case. The subject of the case has to call for a little grin here or there." Adam Liptak, "Justices Call on Bench's Bard to Limit His Lyricism," *New York Times*, December 15, 2002, 41.

23. Quoted in Peter McDonald, *Serious Poetry: Form and Authority from Yeats to Hill* (New York: Oxford University Press, 2007), 87.

24. For instance, X. J. Kennedy observes:

    When you write in rhyme, it's as if you're walking across a series of stepping stones into the darkness, and you can't really see what's at the far end of the stepping stones. So you're led onward, often to say things that surprise and astonish you.

    "X. J. Kennedy," *Fourteen on Form: Conversations with Poets*, ed. William Baer (Jackson: University Press of Mississippi, 2004), 246–247.
    For similar reasons, Donald Davie wrote of rhyme: "Rhyme, of all the tricks that are/In the Muse's repertoire/The most irrational" (*CP*, 224).

25. For instance, in *How Poets See the World: The Art of Description in Contemporary Poetry* (New York: Oxford University Press, 2005), 46, Willard Spiegelman observes, "Rhyme may be either discovery or creation, depending on whether it arrives mysteriously and suddenly or striven for and plotted (and who can ever tell?)."

26. Quoted in Anthony Hecht, *Melodies Unheard: Essays on the Mysteries of Poetry* (Baltimore, MD: Johns Hopkins University Press, 2003), 49–50. Hecht calls Auden's point "almost indisputable."

27. Rakim, "R.A.K.I.M.," *8 Mile Soundtrack* (Interscope Records, 2002).

28. Lupe Fiasco, "Hip Hop Saved My Life," *The Cool* (Atlantic, 2007); hereafter cited in the text as "HH."

29. Lupe Fiasco, "Almost Famous," interview with Kenny Rodriguez, available at http://www.nobodysmiling.com/hiphop/interview/84943.php.

30. Kanye West, "Jesus Walks," *The College Dropout* (Roc-A-Fella, 2004).

31. Lupe Fiasco, "Dumb It Down," *The Cool*; hereafter cited as "DD."

32. Jay-Z, "Ignorant Shit," *American Gangster* (Roc-A-Fella, 2007).

33. Bob Marley, "Trenchtown Rock," *Trenchtown Rock* (Phantom Sound & Vision, 2004).

34. Kanye West, "Crack Music," *Late Registration* (Roc-A-Fella, 2005).

35. Nas, "Carry on Tradition," *Hip Hop Is Dead* (Def Jam, 2006); hereafter cited as "COT."

36. Gordon Braden, *Petrarchan Love and the Continental Renaissance* (New Haven, CT: Yale University Press, 1999), 63.

37. Yung Ralph, "I Work Hard," *Most Unexpected* (Money Maker, 2008).

38. See, for instance, Michael Eric Dyson, *Know What I Mean? Reflections on Hip Hop* (New York: Basic Books, 2007), 64, who dates "the golden age of hip hop" as "from 1987 to 1993."

39. Don DeLillo, *Cosmopolis* (New York: Scribner, 2003), 133; hereafter cited in the text as *C*.

40. Zadie Smith, "The Zen of Eminem," *Vibe*, January 28, 2005, available at http://www.vibe.com/news/magazine_features/2005/01/cover_story_zen_eminem/.

41. Tom Wolfe, *I Am Charlotte Simmons* (New York: Farrar, Straus and Giroux, 2004), 44–45.

42. Dick Davis, *A Trick of Sunlight* (Athens: Swallow Press/Ohio University Press, 2006), 43; hereafter cited in the text as *TS*.

43. I. A. Richards, *Practical Criticism: A Study of Literary Judgment* (New York: Harcourt, Brace and World, 1929), 33; hereafter cited in the text as *PC*.

44. Billy Collins, "A Brief History of the Paradelle," *The Paradelle*, ed. Theresa M. Welford (Los Angeles: Red Hen, 2005), 9; hereafter cited in the text as *TP*.

45. Roger Ide, "The Reader Replies," *American Scholar*, Fall 1997, 173–174.

46. Kanye West, "Gold Digger," *Late Registration* (Roc-A-Fella, 2005).

47. Ray Charles, "'I've Got a Woman," *The Very Best of Ray Charles* (Rhino, 2000). Since the song is more commonly referred to as "I Got a Woman," I follow that convention to minimize confusion.

48. Lisa de Moraes, "Kanye West's Torrent of Criticism, Live on NBC," *Washington Post,* September 3, 2005, C01, available at http://www.washingtonpost.com/wp-dyn/content/article/2005/09/03/AR2005090300165.html.

49. See John Lenand, "Art Born of Outrage in the Internet Age," *New York Times,* September 25, 2005, sec. 4, p. 1; and "Legendary K.O. Press Release," available at http://www.k-otix.com/index.php?option=com_content&task=view&id=43&Itemid=2.

50. George W. Bush, *Decision Points* (New York: Crown Publisher, 2010), 326.

51. The Legendary K.O., "George Bush Don't Like Black People," available at http://revver.com/video/71633/george-bush-dont-like-black-people/.

Chapter 2

1. Elvis Mitchell, "Spike Lee: The *Playboy* Interview," *Spike Lee: Interviews*, ed. Cynthia Fuchs (Jackson: University Press of Mississippi, 2002), 37.

2. Public Enemy, "Fight the Power," *Fear of a Black Planet* (Def Jam, 1990); hereafter cited in the text as "FP."

3. See Peter Guralnick, "How Did Elvis Get Turned into a Racist?" *New York Times*, August 11, 2007, A5.

4. Robert Pinsky, "Dissed in Verse: The Art of the Poetic Insult," Slate, April 26, 2006, available at http://www.slate.com/id/2140565/.

5. Alan Dundes, Jerry W. Leach, and Bora Ozkok, "The Strategy of Turkish Boys' Verbal Dueling Rhymes," *Journal of American Folklore* 83 (July-September 1970): 325–349, provides a classic discussion of the phenomenon of verbal

duels. For a bibliography of "verbal contests," see Barbara Kirshenblatt-Gimblett, "Bibliographic Survey of the Literature of Speech Play and Related Subjects," *Speech Play: Bibliographic Research and Resources for Studying Linguistic Creativity*, ed. Barbara Kirshenblatt-Gimblett (Philadelphia: University of Pennsylvania Press, 1976), 205–206. X. J. Kennedy's anthology *Tygers of Wrath: Poems of Hate, Anger and Invective* (Athens: University of Georgia Press, 1981) includes many intriguing examples from poetry in English and the introduction offers a useful overview of the subject. See also Geoffrey Hughes, *Swearing: A Social History of Foul Language, Oaths, and Profanity in English* (Oxford: Blackwell, 1991), for a lucid discussion of a related field, and Douglas Gary, "Rough Music: Some Early Invectives and Flytings," *Yearbook of English Studies* 14 (1984): 21–43, for a discussion of the phenomenon.

6. Pat Rogers, *The Augustan Vision* (London: Methuen, 1978), 171; and Steven N. Zwicker, "Composing a Literary Life: Introduction," *The Cambridge Companion to John Dryden*, ed. Steven N. Zwicker (Cambridge: Cambridge University Press, 2004), 11.

7. M. Lindsay Kaplan, *The Culture of Slander in Early Modern England* (Cambridge: Cambridge University Press, 1997), 30. See also Kenneth Gross's excellent study, *Shakespeare's Noise* (Chicago: University of Chicago Press, 2001), especially "Introduction" (1–9) and "*King Lear* and the Register of Curse" (161–192).

8. A conspicuous exception is Kent Johnson, who rather forcefully violates these norms. Instead of avoiding enemy making, his work encourages it. In *Epigramititis: 100 Living American Poets* (Kenmore, NY: BlazeVOX, 2004), Johnson laments that "poets these days are, for the most part, strategically polite and scriptedly protocolled toward their peers" (16), then offers one hundred epigrams that attack the most prominent contemporary poets by name.

9. Roman Jakobson, *Selected Writings, Vol. 3: Poetry of Grammar, Grammar of Poetry*, ed. Stephen Rudy (The Hague: Mouton, 1982), 39.

10. Chuck D with Yusuf Jah, *Fight the Power: Rap, Race, and Reality* (New York: Bantam Doubleday, 1997), 196.

11. Arthur Schopenhauer, "The World as Will and Representation," *Continental Aesthetics: Romanticism to Postmodernism: An Anthology*, ed. Richard Kearney and David M. Rasmussen (New York: Blackwell, 2001), 84.

12. Run-D.M.C., "My Adidas," *Raising Hell* (Arista, 1986).

13. I take the term "synonym-rhyme" from Marjorie Perloff, *Rhyme and Meaning in the Poetry of Yeats* (The Hague: Mouton, 1970), 67–71.

14. See David Rieff, "Dangerous Pity," *Prospect*, June 20, 2005, available at http://www.prospect-magazine.co.uk/article_details. php?id=6937.

15. See "Bio," Blowfly, http://www.blowflyofficial.com/bio.html.

16. Blowfly, "Rap Dirty" (twelve-inch single, 1980).

17. Russell Myrie, Don't Rhyme for the Sake of Riddlin': The Authorized Story of Public Enemy (Edinburgh: Canongate, 2008), 124.

18. Bobby McFerrin, *The Best of Bobby McFerrin* (Blue Note Records, 1996).

19. Living Colour, "Elvis Is Dead," *Time's Up* (Sony, 1990).

20. U2 and Brian Eno, "Elvis Ate America," *Passengers: Original Soundtracks 1* (Island, 1985).

21. Thomas W. Talley, *Negro Folk Rhymes: Wise and Otherwise* (New York: Macmillan, 1922), 316.

22. See Dennis Wepman, Ronald B. Newman, and Murray B. Binderman, "Toasts: The New Black Urban Folk Poetry," *Journal of American Folklore* 87, no. 345 (July-September 1974): 208–224; Cornel West, *The Cornel West Reader* (New York: Basic, 1999), 288; and Henry Louis Gates Jr., *The Signifying Monkey: A Theory of Afro-American Literary Criticism* (New York: Oxford University Press, 1988).

23. Daryl Cumber Dance, *From My People: 400 Years of African American Folklore* (New York: W. W. Norton, 2002), 474.

24. The *New York Times*, for example, observed that

    [t]he murder of Yankel Rosenbaum, the acquittal of the youth accused of killing him and the public disorder and failures of

government that Crown Heights came to symbolize, dogged Mayor David N. Dinkins and might have helped to elect Rudolph W. Giuliani.

See Todd S. Pudrum, "Unhealed Wounds of Crown Heights Bared Again," *New York Times*, August 12, 1994, available at http://query.nytimes.com/gst/fullpage.html?res=9A01E1DD15 39F931A2575BC0A962958260&n=Top/Reference/Times%20 Topics/People/R/Rosenbaum,%20Yankel. See also Edward Shapiro, *Crown Heights: Blacks, Jews, and the 1991 Brooklyn Riot* (Waltham, MA: Brandeis University Press, 2006), and, for a participant's perspective, Al Sharpton and Karen Hunter, *Al on America* (New York: Kensington, 2003), 217–222.

25. Joel Seidemann, *In the Interest of Justice: Great Opening and Closing Arguments of the Last 100 Years* (New York: HarperCollins, 2005), 358–359.
26. Constance Hale, Sin and Syntax: How to Craft Wickedly Effective Prose (New York: Random House, 1999), 236, and Robert Mayer, *How to Win Any Argument without Raising Your Voice, Losing Your Cool, or Coming to Blows* (Franklin Lakes, NJ: Career Press, 2005), 172.
27. Johnnie L. Cochran and David Fisher, *A Lawyer's Life* (New York: Macmillan, 2002), 108. Speaking of his rhymes, Cochran observed, "I'd found that juries enjoyed them, understood them, and, most importantly remembered them" (108).
28. Martha Wolfenstein, *Children's Humor: A Psychological Analysis* (Glencoe, IL: Free Press, 1954), 182.
29. NWA, "Fuck tha Police," *Straight Outta Compton* (Ruthless Records, 1988).
30. Yvor Winters, "The Poetry of J. V. Cunningham," *Twentieth Century Literature* 6, no. 4 (1961): 164.
31. Anthony Hecht, from "A Little Cemetery," *Counter/Measures* 1 (1972): 15.
32. Anthony Hecht with Philip Hoy, *Anthony Hecht in Conversation with Philip Hoy* (London: Between the Lines, 1999), 78.
33. Jon Stallworthy, "The Fury and the Mire," *The Oxford Handbook of British and Irish War Poetry*, ed. Tim Kendall (New York: Oxford University Press, 2007), 570.

34. Bizarre featuring Eminem, "Hip Hop," *Hannicap Circus* (Sanctuary, 2005).

35. Veronica Schmidt, "Glastonbury Line-up Leaked," *Times Online*, April 28, 2008, available at http://entertainment.timesonline.co.uk/tol/arts_and_entertainment/music/festivals/article3835041.ece.

36. Jay-Z, "Jockin' Jay-Z (Dope Boy Fresh)," *The Blueprint III* (Roc-A-Fella, 2008); hereafter cited in the text as "JJZ."

37. Capone-N-Noreaga featuring Foxy Brown, "Bang Bang," *The Reunion* (Rhino/Ada, 2000).

38. Lil' Kim, "Came Back for You," *La Bella Mafia* (Atlantic/Wea, 2003); hereafter cited as "CBFY."

39. Fox News, "Hollywood's 20 Tackiest Celebrities," available at http://www.foxnews.com/photoessay/0,4644,6424,00.html# 19_605.

40. Big Daddy Kane, "Ain't No Half Steppin'," *Long Live Kane* (Warner Bros/Wea, 1990), and Boogie Down Productions, "Poetry," *Criminal Minded* (B-Boy Records, 1987).

41. Wu-Tang Clan, "Triumph," *Wu-Tang Forever* (Relativity, 1997).

42. Arthur Schopenhauer, *The World as Will and Idea*, vol. 3, trans. R. B. Haldane and J. Kemps (London: Trubner, 1886), 208.

43. Wyclef Jean, "Masquerade," *Masquerade* (Sony, 2002).

44. T-Pain, "Ringleader Man" (MP3 download).

45. William Butler Yeats, *Mythologies* (Whitefish, MT: Kessinger Publishing Company, 2003), 150; hereafter cited in the text as *M*.

46. W. B. Yeats, *The Collected Poems of W. B. Yeats,* ed. Richard Finneran, 2nd ed. (New York: Simon and Schuster, 1996), 245.

Chapter 3

1. Ne-Yo, "Mirror," *In My Own Words* (Def Jam, 2006).

2. Ne-Yo, "Bang Bang" (unreleased track).

3. The Pierces, "Boring," *Thirteen Tales of Love and Revenge* (Lizard King Records, 2007); hereafter cited in the text as "B."

4. Missy Elliot, "Work It," *Under Construction* (Goldmind/Elektra, 2002).

5. Afroman, "Whack Rappers," *Afroholic.. The Even Better Times* (reissue, Hungry Hustler, 2004).

6. Octavio Paz, *The Double Flame: Love and Eroticism*, trans. Helen Lane (New York: Harcourt, Brace, 1993), 3.

7. Run-D.M.C., "King of Rock," *King of Rock* (Profile/Arista Records, 1985).

8. John Flurio, *Second Frutes*, ed. R. C. Simonini Jr. (Gainesville, FL: Scholars' Facsimiles and Reprints, 1953), 2–3. For a brief discussion of this passage, see Stephen Burt and David Mikics, *The Art of the Sonnet* (Cambridge: Harvard University Press, 2010), 12.

9. William Shakespeare, *The Oxford Shakespeare: The Complete Works,* ed. John Jowett, William Montgomery, Gary Taylor, and Stanley Wells, 2nd ed. (New York: Oxford University Press, 2005), 591; hereafter cited in the text as *TOS*. See also Paul Fussell, *Poetic Meter and Poetic Form* (New York: McGraw-Hill, 1979), 112, where he observes that "[a]lthough our age seems to have lost the sense that rhyme betokens 'accord,' in the Renaissance the idea was a rich commonplace, with impressive erotic advantage to writers like Spenser."

10. W. H. Auden, *The Collected Works of W. H. Auden: Prose 1939–1948*, ed. Edward Mendelson (London: Faber and Faber, 2002), 346.

11. Marjorie Garber, *Shakespeare after All* (New York: Random House, 2004), 179.

12. Nelly Furtado, "Promiscuous," featuring Timbaland, *Loose* (Mosley, 2006); hereafter cited in the text as "P."

13. I take this phrase from Anne Carson's *Eros the Bittersweet*, which stresses how desire separates lovers. "Eros is in between," she observes, explaining the particular geometric relations that this dynamic inspires, what she calls "the radical constitution of desire:

> For, where eros is lack, its activation calls for three structural components—lover, beloved, and that which comes between them. They are three points of transformation on a circuit of possible relationship, electrified by desire so that they touch not touching. Conjoined they are held apart.

See Anne Carson, *Eros the Bittersweet* (Princeton: Princeton University Press, 1986), 109, 16. As I suggest, hip-hop seduction verse emphasizes the opposite force.

14. Rob Sheffield, *Love Is a Mix Tape: Life and Loss, One Song at a Time* (New York: Crown, 2007), 218.

15. Sherman Alexie, *War Dances* (New York: Grove, 2009), 183.

16. The Bloodhound Gang, "The Bad Touch," *Hooray for Boobies* (Interscope, 2000).

17. LL Cool J, "Hey Lover," *Mr. Smith* (Def Jam, 1985).

18. LL Cool J, "Rock the Bells," *Radio* (Def Jam, 1985).

19. LL Cool J, "Pink Cookies in a Plastic Bag Getting Crushed by Buildings," *14 Shots to the Dome* (Def Jam, 1993).

20. *Eve Kosofsky Sedgwick, Between Men: English Literature and Male Homosocial Desire (New York: Columbia University Press, 1985), 80; hereafter cited in the text as BMEL.*

21. LL Cool J with Karen Hunter, *I Make My Own Rules* (New York: St. Martin's, 1997), 156.

22. Big Daddy Kane, "Very Special," *Looks Like a Job For...* (Cold Chillin'/Reprise/Warner Brothers, 1993); hereafter cited in the text as "VS."

23. Big Daddy Kane, "All of Me," *A Taste of Chocolate* (Cold Chillin'/Reprise/Warner Brothers, 1990). The opening banter appears in the video; hereafter cited in the text as "AOM."

24. Eminem, "Seduction," *Recovery* (Aftermath, 2010); hereafter cited in the text as "S."

25. Snoop Dogg, "Sexual Eruption," *Ego Trippin'* (Doggystyle, 2007).

26. Richard Hugo, *The Triggering Town: Lectures and Essays on Poetry and Writing* (New York: W. W. Norton, 1979), 32.

27. Eminem, "Yellow Brick Road," *Encore* (Aftermath, 2004). Rap Genius first called this reference to my attention.

28. Eminem, "Still Don't Give a Fuck," *The Slim Shady LP* (Aftermath, 1999); hereafter cited in the text as "Still."

29. John Hollander, *Rhyme's Reason: A Guide to English Verse*, 3rd ed. (New Haven, CT: Yale University Press, 2000), 14.

30. M. H. Abrams and Geoffrey Galt Harpham, *A Glossary of Literary Terms* (Boston: Wadsworth, 2012), 349.

31. George Puttenham, *The Art of English Poesy: A Critical Edition*, ed. Frank Whigham and Wayne A. Rebhorn (Ithaca: Cornell University Press, 2007), 133.

Chapter 4

1. Kevin Young, "Expecting," *The New Yorker*, January 3, 2011, 43; hereafter cited in the text as "E."
2. Rafael Campo, *Landscape with Human Figure* (Durham, NC: Duke University Press, 2002), 55 and *The Enemy* (Durham, NC: Duke University Press, 2002), 10.
3. In addition to other works and individual poems specifically discussed here, other notable examples include the following collections: Michael Cirelli, *Lobster with Ol' Dirty Bastard* (Brooklyn, NY: Hanging Loose Press, 2008); Kevin Coval, *L-vis Lives! Racemusic Poems* (Chicago: Haymarket Books, 2011); Thomas Sayers Ellis, *The Maverick Room* (Saint Paul, MN: Graywolf Press, 2005); Ed-Bok Lee, *Real Karaoke People* (Moorhead, MN: New Rivers Press, 2005); Adrian Matejka, *Mixology* (New York: Penguin 2009); Eugene Ostashevsky, *The Life and Opinions of DJ Spinoza* (Brooklyn, NY: Ugly Duckling Presse, 2008); and Marcus Wicker, *Maybe the Saddest Thing* (New York: HarperCollins, 2012). See also *Bestiary: A Magazine of Poetry and Art*, Issue 2, Hip-Hop, 2011. An interesting subgenre of poems that critique hip hop also has developed, some more informed than others. See, for instance, A. Van Jordan, "R & B," *Quantum Lyrics* (New York: W. W. Norton, 2007), 104–108; Geoffrey Hill's address to "RAPMASTER," the "evil twin," in *Speech! Speech!* (Washington, DC: Counterpoint, 2000), 46–48; and Tony Hoagland, "Rap Music," *What Narcissism Means to Me* (Saint Paul, MN: Graywolf Press, 2003), 49–50.
4. John Murilo, *Up Jump the Boogie* (New York: Cypher, 2010), 23; hereafter cited in the text as *UJB*.
5. Michael Robbins, *Alien vs. Predator* (New York: Penguin, 2012), 69; hereafter cited in the text as *AVP*.
6. Emily Witt, "Michael Robbins on 'Alien vs. Predator,'" *Paris Review Daily*, March 27, 2012, hereafter cited as "MR," available at http://www.theparisreview.org/blog/2012/03/27/michael-robbins-on-%E2%80%98alien-vs-predator%E2%80%99/.

7. Kevin Young, *The Gray Album: On the Blackness of Blackness* (Minneapolis, MN: Graywolf Press, 2012), 337.

8. "An Interview with Former USA National Poetry Series Winner Adrian Matejka [Culturelicious]," *Racialicious*, March 12, 2012, available at http://www.racialicious.com/2012/03/12/an-interview-with-former-usa-national-poetry-series-winner-adrian-matejka-culturelicious/.

9. Matthew Dickman, *All-American Poem* (Philadelphia: American Poetry Review, 2008), 42; hereafter cited in the text as *AAP*.

10. Campbell McGrath, *Pax Atomica* (New York: HarperCollins, 2004), 48; hereafter cited in the text as *PA*.

11. Stephen Burt, *The Forms of Youth: Twentieth-Century Poetry and Adolescence* (New York: Columbia University Press, 2007), 196. For an illuminating consideration of the connection between contemporary poetry and music, see Jahan Ramazani, "'Sing to Me Now': Contemporary American Poetry and Song,'" *Contemporary Literature* 52, no. 4 (2011): 716–755.

12. Jay-Z, "Allure," *The Black Album* (Rock-A-Fella, 2003).

13. James Longenbach, "Poetic Compression," *New England Review* 32, no. 1 (2011): 165.

14. Andrew Ross, "The Death of Lady Day," *Frank O'Hara: To Be True to a City*, ed. Jim Elledge (Ann Arbor: University of Michigan Press, 1990), 386.

15. Joe LeSueur, *Digressions on Some Poems by Frank O'Hara: A Memoir* (New York: Farrar, Straus and Giroux, 2003), 38.

16. Tricia Rose, *The Hip Hop Wars: What We Talk about When We Talk about Hip Hop—and Why It Matters* (New York: Basic, 2008), 232. For a more extended discussion of this subject that draws different conclusions, see Bakari Kitwana, *Why White Kids Love Hip-Hop* (New York: Basic, 2005).

17. Erica Dawson, *Big-Eyed Afraid* (Ewell, Surrey: Waywiser Press, 2007), 31; hereafter cited in the text as *BEA*.

18. Ralph Ellison, *Shadow and Act* (New York: Vintage, 1972), 222.

19. Kurtis Blow, "Tough," *Tough* (Mercury Records, 1982); Ice Cube, "Urbanian," *I Am the West* (Lench Mob, 2010).

20. Dave Hollander, *52 Weeks: Interviews with Champions!* (Guilford, CT: Lyons Press, 2006), 10; hereafter cited in the text as *WIWC*.

21. Tom Friend, "Old College Try," *The Best American Sports Writing 2011*, ed. Jane Leavy and Glenn Stout (New York: Mariner, 2012), 217.

22. Darryl Dawkins and Charley Rosen, *Chocolate Thunder: The Uncensored Life and Times of the NBA's Original Showman* (Toronto: Sports Classic, 2003), 94.

23. John Edgar Wideman, the novelist and former all-Ivy forward, adds a useful distinction between "showmanship" and "showboating":

    showmanship (profiling, styling his play to enhance and personalize the action, make it more fun, more challenging, more impressive, while not interfering with, maybe even forwarding, the purpose of the game: to provide an opportunity for ten people to work hard, work well at winning, consciously respectful of the game's traditions) or showboating (calling attention to himself as if the game's only about him, about accumulating his own individual style points, damn the score, the game, everybody else on the court, now yesterday, or whenever).

    As Wideman admits, the two styles remain difficult to distinguish. Vexed by a particular player, for instance, Wideman puzzles over how to categorize him and, ultimately, he cannot decide whether he watches a "cartoon version of basketball ultimately destructive for players and the game" or "[t]he no-man's-land of innovation." See John Edgar Wideman, *Hoop Roots: Basketball, Race, and Love* (Boston: Houghton Mifflin, 2001), 182, 183.

24. Charles Kingsley, "Tennyson" (1850)," *Alfred Lord Tennyson*, ed. Paul Fox (New York: Infobase, 2010), 62.

25. Christopher Ricks, *Tennyson*, 2nd ed. (Berkeley: University of California Press, 1989), 216.

26. George Saintsbury, *A History of English Prosody from the Twelfth Century to the Present Day*, vol. 3 (London: Macmillan, 1910), 205.

27. Erica Dawson, email to author, June 20, 2011.

28. James Wood, *The Irresponsible Self: On Laughter and the Novel* (New York: Farrar, Straus and Giroux, 2004), 178.

29. Indeep, "Last Night a DJ Saved My Life," *Last Night a DJ Saved My Life* (Sound of New York/Becket Records, 1982). More faintly, Robbins's line also borrows from the title of The Hold Steady's album, *Almost Killed Me* (Frenchkiss, 2004).

30. "What Is Rap Genius," Rap Genius, available at http://rapgenius.com/static/about. See also "Understanding Rap," available at http://understandrap.com/.

31. See http://rapgenius.com/Drake-the-motto-lyrics.

32. Shadowcast, "'Don't Ask Me How': The Elusive Triple Entendre in Hip-Hop," Rap Genius, undated, available at http://rapgenius.com/posts/Don-t-ask-me-how-the-elusive-triple-entendre-in-hip-hop.

33. Thomas Nagel, "What Is It Like to Be a Bat?" *Philosophical Review* 83, no. 4 (1974): 439.

34. Richard Wilbur, *New and Collected Poems* (New York: Mariner, 1988), 240.

35. Michael Robbins, "Are You Smeared with the Juice of Cherries?" *Poetry*, September 2010, 44; hereafter cited in the text as "AYS."

36. Major Jackson, *Hoops* (New York: W. W. Norton, 2006), 85; hereafter cited in the text as *H*.

37. W. H. Auden, *Collected Poems*, ed. Edward Mendelson (New York: Random House, 2007), 84.

38. For instance, like Auden in "Letter to Lord Byron," Jackson debates what manner of address he should use, and he describes the physical posture he employs when writing.

39. Major Jackson, liner notes for The Roots, *Do You Want More?!!!??!* (Geffen Records, 1995).

40. James C. Hall, *Mercy, Mercy Me: African-American Culture and the American Sixties* (New York: Oxford University Press, 2001), 51.

41. Kevin Bezner, "A Life Distilled: An Interview with Gwendolyn Brooks," *Conversations with Gwendolyn Brooks* (Jackson: University Press of Mississippi, 2003), 120;

Conversations with Gwendolyn Brooks hereafter cited in the text as *CGB*.

42. Hoyt Fuller, Eugenia Collier, George Kent, Dudley Randall, in *CGB*, 68.

43. Sonia Sanchez, *Does Your House Have Lions?* (Boston: Beacon Press, 1997).

44. Thomas Sayers Ellis, *The Maverick Room* (Saint Paul, MN: Graywolf Press, 2005), 6.

45. Coval, *L-vis Lives!* 15.

46. Terrance Hayes, *Wind in a Box* (New York: Penguin, 2006), 40.

47. Terrance Hayes, *Hip Logic* (New York: Penguin, 2002), 5.

48. Ibid.

49. D. A. Powell, *Tea* (Middleton, CT: Wesleyan University Press, 1988), 13; hereafter cited in the text as *T*.

50. See Jasha Hoffman, "'Cocktails' For Two: Interview with D. A. Powell," *Harvard Crimson*, November 9, 2001, available at http://www.thecrimson.com/article/2001/11/9/cocktails-for-two-interview-with-da/.

51. D. A. Powell, *Cocktails* (Minneapolis, MN: Graywolf Press, 2004), 4; hereafter cited in the text as *C*.

52. Robert Frost, *The Robert Frost Reader: Poetry and Prose*, ed. Edward Connery Lathem and Lawrance Thompson (New York: Henry Holt, 1972), 144. Florio is quoted in Charles Mahoney, "The Temptation of Tercets," *A Companion to Romantic Poetry*, ed. Charles Mahoney (Oxford: Wiley-Blackwell, 2011), 46.

53. Grandmaster Flash and the Furious Five, "The Message," *The Message* (Sugar Hill Records, 1982).

54. Sugar Hill Gang, "Rapper's Delight," *Sugar Hill Gang* (Sugar Hill Records, 1980).

55. Daniel Kane, *What Is Poetry: Conversations with the American Avant-Garde* (New York: T&W, 2003), 129.

56. Big Daddy Kane, "Smooth Operator," *It's a Big Daddy Thing* (Cold Chillin'/Warner Brothers, 1989).

57. James Fenton, *An Introduction to English Poetry* (New York: Farrar, Straus and Giroux, 2002), 94.

Conclusion

1. Thomas Pinney, ed., *The Letters of Rudyard Kipling*, vol. 4 (Iowa City: University of Iowa Press, 1999), 33–34, contains the relevant portions of both versions as well as Kipling's letter to Matthews; hereafter cited in the text as *LRK*.

2. Rudyard Kipling, *The Writings in Prose and Verse of Rudyard Kipling*, vol. 21, *The Five Nations* (New York: Charles Scribner's Sons, 1903), 20.

3. Brander Matthews, *A Study of Versification* (Boston: Houghton Mifflin, 1911), 52–53.

4. Dylan Thomas, *The Poems*, ed. Daniel Jones (London: J. M. Dent and Sons, 1990), 84.

5. T. V. F. Brogan, "Near Rhyme," *The Princeton Encyclopedia of Poetry and Poetics*, ed. Roland Greene (Princeton, NJ: Princeton University Press, 2012), 925.

6. See, for instance, Anne Ferry, *By Design: Intention in Poetry* (Stanford, CA: Stanford University Press, 2008), especially the chapters, "*Love* Rhymes with *Of*" and "The Sense of a Rhyme"; J. Paul Hunter, "Formalism and History: Binarism and the Anglophone Couplet," *Modern Language Quarterly* 6, no. 1 (2000): 109–129; Hugh Kenner, "Rhyme: An Unfinished Monograph" in *Common Knowledge* 10.3 (2004) 377–425; Adela Pinch, "Rhyme's End," *Victorian Studies* 53, no. 3 (2011): 485–494; Kyle Pivetti, "Coupling Past and Future: Dryden's Rhymes as History," *Modern Philology* 109, no. 1 (2011): 85–107; and David Scott Wilson-Okamura, "The French Aesthetic of Spenser's Feminine Rhyme," *Modern Language Quarterly* 68, no. 3 (2007): 345–362.

7. Jay-Z, *Decoded* (New York: Spiegel and Grau, 2010), 17.

8. Ibid.

9. Rob Kenner, "13 Ways of Looking at a White Boy," *Vibe,* June/July 1991, 118.

10. Ice-T featuring The Glove, "Reckless" (PolyGram Records, 1984).

11. Nas, "Memory Lane (Sittin' in da Park)," *Illmatic* (Columbia Records, 1994).

12. Michel Jean-Baptiste et al., "Quantitative Analysis of Culture Using Millions of Digitized Books," *Science* 331 (2011): 176; hereafter cited in the text as "QAC."

13. See L. Rhodes, "Syntax Idols," *Culture Ramp*, September 3, 2012, available at http://cultureramp.com/syntax-idols/.

14. Alexander M. Petersen, Joel Tenenbaum, Shlomo Havlin, and H. Eugene Stanley, "Statistical Laws Governing Fluctuations in Word Use from Word Birth to Word Death," *Scientific Report* 2, article number 313, March 15, 2012, 4; hereafter cited in the text as "SLGF."

15. Lupe Fiasco, "Popular Demand," *Enemy of the State: A Love Story* (mixtape).

16. Anne Ferry, "*Love* Rhymes with *Of*," *Modernism/Modernity* 7, no. 3, 2000: 424.

17. Sir Philip Sidney, *Selected Poetry and Prose*, ed. Robert Kimbrough (Madison: University of Wisconsin Press, 1983), 154–155. See also Ferry, *By Design*, 37.

18. See Robyn Creswell, "The Poem Stuck in My Head: Thomas Sayers Ellis's 'Or,'" *Paris Review Daily*, January 12, 2012, available at http://www.theparisreview.org/blog/2012/01/12/or/.

INDEX